The *Adve*
of Sir Samuel Tuke

It was the ultimate amateur triumph – the soldier-courtier came
from nowhere to write for his king the first smash hit
of Restoration theatre

ALRA
www.alra.co.uk

FOR JACK MITCHLEY

ACKNOWLEDGEMENTS

My grateful thanks to Albert Austin, Mary Nyman and Fred Popely for technical help in preparing this book for the press.
P.M.S.H.

The *Adventures* of Sir Samuel Tuke

Edited and with an introduction by
Paul M.S. Hopkins

FULL AUTHENTIC TEXT OF TUKE'S PLAY
AND SUGGESTIONS FOR STAGING
THE ADVENTURES OF FIVE HOURS

ITURI

Published 2003 by Ituri Publications
4 Chestnut Close
Woodford Halse
Northants NN11 3NB (UK)

ISBN 0 9536430 4 2

Introduction text set in Class Garamound 11/13 point and play set in
Monotype Times New Roman 11/13 pt by Book Production Services, London

Printed in Great Britain by Antony Rowe Ltd

Cover design by Book Production Services, London

A CIP catalogue record for this book is available from the British Library

Front cover illustration: The Laughing Audience (detail), by William Hogarth

CONTENTS

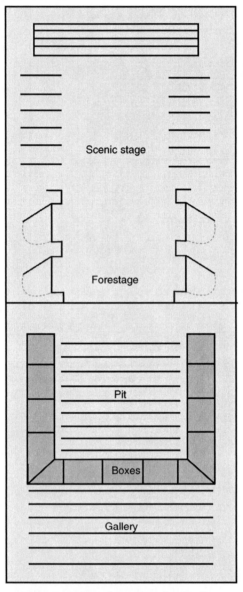

The Duke's Theatre, Lincoln's Inn Fields, 1663,
where *The Adventures* was first performed

PROLOGUE

AN English version of the Spanish tragi-comedy *The Complications of Six Hours* was the idea of Charles the Second. The soldier-courtier who undertook the task had never written a play (and was never to write another). Yet, shorn of an hour in the translation, it became the first smash hit of the post-1660 theatre.

'Everyone' was at the first night on January 8 1663. Pepys was in raptures. Evelyn thought the plot 'incomparable' but was less sure about the language.

The play set a record for the number of consecutive performances which lasted for the rest of the century, during which the plays of Dryden, Etherege, Congreve and Wycherley which are now studied and staged as the cream of 'Restoration' theatre first appeared with less success.

These later dramatists did not drive *The Adventures* from the stage. The play was often revived in the public theatres and at court for the next 50 years; it was adapted to suit the changed tastes of 18th and 19th century audiences: and it was in print for over 250 years.

Then it vanished. The play has no recent stage history. And no text in a format suitable for use in the theatre has been published for 75 years.

This edition aims to fill the publishing gap, with a full history of the *The Adventures* and of its author, Samuel Tuke, whose subsequent knighthood and baronetcy must owe something to his improbable success as a dramatist.

The text is reprinted in the third edition of 1671, for which the by-then Sir Samuel revised and corrected it, taking hints from Dryden in the process. The spelling has been modernised, and notes on production possibilities added. My hope is that *The Adventures of Five Hours* will now return not only to the bookshelf but also to the stage, where 340 years ago it began – and where I believe it belongs today.

1: A MIGHTY GOOD PLAY

There is little doubt which play that inveterate theatregoer Samuel Pepys placed top of his list.

On August 15 1666, Pepys did the equivalent of commuting to work. He went by boat to the naval dockyards, passing the time with a book.

'So down the river, reading *The Adventures of Five Hours*, which the more I read the more I admire,' he confided to his diary. Five days later he made the trip again: 'Up and to Deptford by water, reading *Othello, Moore of Venice*, which I ever heretofore esteemed a mighty good play; but having so lately read *The Adventures of Five Hours*, it seems a mean thing.'

'This curious judgement has both damaged Pepys's credit as a critic and left scholars wary of Tuke's play,' as a scholar put it a few years ago.

Pepys wasn't writing as a critic or scholar - his private diary was for his own edification. This judgement, however eccentric, represented an opinion arrived at on the basis of substantial knowledge.

Pepys was doing a lot of play-reading in 1666 because theatregoing had been interrupted by the plague. He had seen Samuel Tuke's tragi-comedy at least twice. And he had read it before. He bought a copy in 1663, as soon as it became available.

'After dinner, up and read part of the new play of The Five Hours Adventures; which though I have seen it twice, yet I never did admire or understand it enough - it being a play of the greatest plot that I ever expect to see, and of great vigour quite through the whole play, from beginning to the end,' he noted on May 31 of that year.

The next morning 'begun again to rise betimes, by 4 a-clock, and made an end of *The Adventures of Five Hours*, and it is a most excellent play,' the diarist wrote. To have got up at 4am to finish anything suggests that it was a good read, as well as a good play on the stage.

The first of the performances which Pepys attended at the Duke's Theatre in Lincoln's Inn Fields was the opening night, January 8 1663. He went to extraordinary lengths to make sure of being there. 'Dined at home, and there being the famous new play acted the first time today, which is called *The Adventures of five houres,* at the Duke's house, being they say made or translated by Colonel Tuke, I did long to see it and so made my wife to get her ready, though we were forced to send for a smith to break open her Trunk, her maid Jane being gone forth with the keys.

'And so we went; and though early, were forced to sit almost out of sight at the end of one of the lower forms, so full was the house.' Pepys was not complaining that he couldn't see the stage, but that other people would not notice he was there.

'And the play, in one word, is the best, for the variety and the most excellent continuance of the plot to the very end, that ever I saw or think ever shall. And all possible, not only to be done in that time, but in most other respects very admittable and without one word of ribaldry.

'And the house, by its frequent plaudits, did show their sufficient approbation. So home, with much ado in an hour getting a coach home; and after writing letters at my office, I went home to supper and to bed - now resolving to set up my rest as to plays until Easter, if not Whitsuntime next, excepting plays at court.'

But it was no good. He couldn't stay away. On January 19, 'I took...coach to the Duke's playhouse, where we did see the *Five hours* entertainment again which indeed is a very fine play: though, through my being out of order, it did not seem so good as at first; but I could discern it was not any fault of the play.'

Normally, he would not have had this opportunity to revisit a play after 11 days. Most plays in the 1660s received a maximum of three consecutive performances. Tuke's play broke the pattern of frequent changes of bill, being played six days a week from January 8 to January 22, 13 performances in all. The total stood as a record for the rest of the century,

The 'other' diarist of the period, John Evelyn, was also at that first night and confirms the success of the play - though he is more guarded on its merits.

'I went to see Sir S. Tuke (my kinsman's) Comedy acted at the Dukes Theatre, which so universally took as it was acted for some weeks every day, and 'twas believed it would be worth the Comedians [Davenant's company] 4 or 5000 pounds: Indeed the plot was incomparable but the language stiff and formal'.

Evelyn's figure for the profits sounds over-optimistic. Thirteen full houses at Lincoln's Inn Fields would have meant the play was seen by some 7,500 people, but not paying anything like this amount for the pleasure. There were also fees for acting the play elsewhere but, as we shall see, a special performance for lawyers earned the Comedians only £20.

Evelyn's diary was, more properly, called by him a 'memoir'. It was not written up contemporaneously, as this entry (dated January 8 1663 but saying 'what happened afterwards') makes plain.

The play's success, both artistically and commercially, went into the record books. John Downes reported in his 1708 book *Roscius Anglicanus*, or an Historical Review of the Stage, that 'this play being clothed so Excellently Fine in Proper Habits, and Acted so justly well...it took Successively 13 days together, no other play intervening'.

What was the secret of such success? One factor must have been the way in which it came to be written. It was, in an important sense, by royal command.

A 'prologue at court' which appears in the 1663 first edition explains:

> The author...chanced to hear his Majesty once say
> he lik'd this Plot: he staid: and writ the Play;
> So should Obsequious Subjects catch the Minds
> Of Princes...

In case the point was not taken, Samuel Tuke supplied a marginal note: This refers to the Author's purpose of Retirement, at that time when his Majesty recommended this Plot to him.

Charles the Second had probably read the Spanish play in the edition printed in Madrid in 1657. His love of such drama may have begun with his exile in the Spanish Netherlands, where he acquired his first smattering of the language from a Spanish New

Testament. Tuke, who shared his exile, reported in 1660 that Charles 'understands Spanish' - very necessary if he wanted to sort out the plot of *The Adventures* in the original tongue! His interest, once roused, continued throughout his life. Over 20 years later, in 1685, he commissioned John Crowne to write another comedy, *Sir Courtly Nice*, from a Spanish text which he supplied.

Tuke did, in fact, 'retire' to the country to write the play, and returned with something of which he was very proud. As he put it in his prologue for the public theatre:

> The *English Stage* ne'er had so New a Play.
> The Dress, the Authour, and the Scenes are New.
> This ye have seen before ye'l say; 'tis true;
> But tell me, Gentlemen, who ever saw
> A deep Intrigue confin'd to Five Hours Law,
> Such as for close Contrivance yields to none.

Evelyn provides a clue to how the play had already become 'famous' (as Pepys calls it) before the opening night, and also to how it came to be 'acted so justly well' (as Downes puts it). On December 23 1662 he went with the author 'to hear the Comedians (the leading players of the age including Thomas and Mary Betterton) con and repeat his new comedy...a play whose plot was taken out of the famous poet, Calderon'.

No deception was involved in the claim that the play was from Calderon. It had appeared under his name in the 1657 edition mentioned above. By the 20th century the authorship had been challenged, but at the time there was no reason not to stress Calderon's name in publicity.

Evelyn's visit to a rehearsal has been misinterpreted. William Armstrong, contributing editor on theatre to the major edition of Pepys' Diary, qualifies the January 8 'first time today' reference, calling it 'one of the earliest records of a performance, though Evelyn had seen it on December 23'.

There is a world of difference between conning the lines and performing them. But for the play to be in rehearsal and the lines able to be 'repeated' a fortnight before the first night must have been unusual for the 1660s.

In fact, it looks highly probable that the play was in preparation earlier still. The first edition begins: 'The prologue enters with a play-bill in his hand, and reads, "This day being the 15th of December, shall be acted a new play, never played before, called *The Adventures of Five Hours*".'

If this was the deadline given by the Duke's Company to Tuke - and most authors need a deadline if they are ever to let go of their masterwork - it allowed plenty of time before the 'real' first night in which to prepare the parts and pass them round to be 'conned'.

In addition to performances for the public at Lincoln's Inn Fields, the Duke's Company also performed regularly at Whitehall, for the court. The question 'when did Charles first see the play he had commissioned?' has been much debated.

It is tempting to suggest that it was over Christmas or New Year, before the scrum in which Pepys and Evelyn got involved on January 8. This would give another reason why the play was already 'famous'. But both diarists were adept at getting into court performances and neither mentions one for Adventures at this period. Some respected writers on the theatre in this period have plumped for a royal premiere on December 15 1662, despite no court performance being listed for that day by the Lord Chamberlain.

Eleanore Boswell, in *Restoration Court Stage* wonders whether a new stage being put up in the Great Hall, between the Banqueting House and the river at Whitehall, was 'built for the production of *The Adventures of Five Hours*'. Her chosen date is December 15, solely on the basis of the prologue. But her account of carpenters and others not getting the hall ready until the end of January 1663 argues against the hall being used in December.

On the other hand, Evelyn recalls seeing Dryden's first play, *The Wild Gallant*, 'at the Great Hall at Court, where his Majesty, Queen &c danced', on February 5. The circumstantial detail makes it highly probable he was recalling the event in the right setting. And if so, another play which the Lord Chamberlain records as being performed by the Duke's Company on February 9 seems likely to have been staged there, before the carpenters returned in mid-February because the throne provided for the king was unsatisfactory.

King Charles wrote to his sister on February 9, saying 'I am just now called for to go to the play' but, like the Lord Chamberlain, not naming it. What he told his sister about the play (and the unsatisfactory throne) has not survived. A pity, because this could well have been the first court performance of *The Adventures*.

Staging the play for its royal sponsor after the public run would explain the words 'at length' in the 'epilogue at court':

'We have passed the Lords, and Commons, and are come
At length, dread Sir, to hear your final Doom.
Tis true, your Vassals, Sir, may vote the Laws,
Their Sanction comes from your Divine Applause.
This shining Circle then will all sit mute,
Till one pronounce from you Le Roy le Veut.'

Court etiquette requires the king to begin the clapping. 'Passing the Lords and Commons' sounds like a reference to the successful public performances before, at length, the players were summoned to court. As to 'the Lords', it would also have followed a performance at the Temple on February 2. The custom of holding plays in the Inns of Court at Candlemas was long established. *Twelfth Night* had its first recorded performance in the Middle Temple Hall in 1602. Not surprisingly, in view of its current popularity, *The Adventures* was the 1663 choice.

Pepys reported how he had gone 'to the Temple, where at my cousin Rogers' chamber I met Madam Turner, and after a little stay led her home and there left her, she and her daughter having been at the play today at the Temple, it being a Revelling Time with them.'

What the ladies thought of it Pepys does not record. But some idea of the atmosphere can be gleaned from the prologue written by Sir William Davenant, manager of the company, for the occasion. In the place of honour sat the Lord Chancellor (Lord Clarendon), and on both sides of the hall sat as many as could crowd in for this annual event:

'My lord, you in your early youth did sit
As patron and as Censor too of wit,
When only that which you approved could please

In theatres, the muses' Palaces.
As you were then our Judge, so now we come
In yearly trial to receive our doom...
We Spaniards fight with swords which are too long
To show the art of Fencing in a throng...
When our Don Henrique gainst Octavio draws,
Both may incur the danger of your law,
For wanting space to traverse here the ground,
Missing themselves they may spectators wound.
Though, noble gentlemen, it long hast bin
Your special privilege to hedge us in,
Yet quit that ancient privelege today
And venture not your lives to spoil a play.'

The Temple authorities paid the Duke's Company the standard
£20 fee for the performance, but Davenant's prologue reflects
the expectation of a bumper audience - the play was already a
famously successful 'draw'.

2: THE AUTHOR

The theatre into which Samuel Tuke made his solitary excursion as dramatist was in real need of him.

It was 20 years since the theatres had been closed by the Puritans. Plays went on being published, but not performed, at least with the knowledge of the authorities. The best-known exception to this was *The Siege of Rhodes*, Sir William Davenant's opera, staged privately in 1656, and publicly as soon as the theatres could reopen.

Davenant and his fellow patentee Thomas Killigrew had both written plays before the closure and were able to revive them, together with plays by Shakespeare (shared between the two companies), John Fletcher and other dramatists of the Elizabethan, Jacobean and Caroline periods.

But new work was less easy to find. John Dryden's first play *The Wild Gallant* was staged a month after *The Adventures*, but was not well received. *The Conquest of Granada*, his first successful play, followed in 1664, as did George Etherege's *The Comical Revenge, or Love in a Tub*.

Three of the five plays now most staged and studied as 'Restoration' - Wycherley's *The Country Wife* and *The Plain Dealer* and Etherege's The *Man of Mode* - came more than a dozen years after *The Adventures*, while Congreve's *Love for Love* and *The Way of the World* were first staged in the reign of William and Mary.

There would have been a market from 1660 for translations and adaptations of Moliere's plays - courtiers had seen them while in exile. But it was not until the middle of 1663 that Davenant led the way with *The Playhouse to be Let*, to be followed by a flood of English plays for which dramatists purloined characters and situations from the French master.

At the beginning of 1663, the field was clear for Tuke to show what could he could do with a Spanish original, of the type from which Moliere and his French fellow-dramatists themselves borrowed. He took that opportunity superbly.

The Dictionary of National Biography (and others following it) describes Samuel Tuke as 'third son of George Tuke of Frayling, Essex', a misreading of the Register of Grays Inn, where Samuel and his elder brother George enrolled in 1635. The parish register for Frating, near Colchester, confirms that George Tuke lived there in the 1630s, but there is no trace of any of his children being born in Frating. It is far more likely that they were born at Layer Marney, ten miles away, though the early registers for this parish have not survived.

Layer Marney Tower, one of the great houses of Essex, was among the properties acquired by Samuel's great-great-grandfather from the proceeds of service to an earlier monarch.

Bryan Tuke, a lawyer and Sheriff of Essex, became secretary to Cardinal Wolsey, then steward and treasurer to King Henry VIII. He evidently did well out of the connections, acquiring a knighthood, building a mansion at South Weald and purchasing Layer Marney Tower as well as properties elsewhere in Essex and in Hertfordshire. Sir Bryan, whose civil service achievements include setting up a postal system along main roads, initially for royal despatches but later available to everyone, died in 1545.

A family tree drawn up in 1931 by E.S. de Beer, editor of a modern edition of Pepys, provides the link, via a George (died 1573) whose widow entertained Queen Elizabeth at Layer Marney; then Peter, who sold the great house but whose son, Samuel's father George, kept the tenancy of part of the estate, according to the Essex historian Philip Morant.

De Beer makes Samuel the fourth son, with George the third. The DNB and de Beer agree, however, that their father married Elizabeth, daughter of Christopher Wase, a London goldsmith.

After enrolling at Grays Inn, Samuel Tuke next appeared in the record when the civil war broke out. He entered the king's army and fought at Marston Moor and elsewhere, becoming a colonel of horse. He resigned over a quarrel with another officer, but rejoined and took part in the defence of Colchester, nearest town to Frating, in 1648.

He acted as one of the commissioners for the besieged when

the town capitulated to the Parliamentarians, and was bitter about the way the defenders were treated. After the Restoration in 1660, John Evelyn recalls hearing Tuke's account to the House of Lords 'of the transaction at Colchester in murdering in cold blood Lord Capel, and the rest of those brave men, that suffered in cold blood, after articles of rendition'.

But between 1648 and the Restoration, Tuke spent most of his time on the continent. Evelyn first met 'cousin Tuke' at Padua in 1649. In 1657 Queen Henrietta recommended him as secretary to the Duke of York (the future King James) but Edward Hyde, Lord Clarendon, persuaded Charles that Tuke was 'in no way fit for the office'. About this time, Tuke became a Roman Catholic, which may explain Hyde's action.

In preparation for the king's return to England, a 'Character of Charles the Second written by an Impartial Hand', attributed to Tuke, was 'exposed to Public View for the Information of the People' on April 30 1660, four weeks before Charles himself landed.

This piece of seventeenth century public relations bent the truth a little - the author talks about 'my return to England after Eleven years' absence', glossing over a visit he paid to Evelyn 'out of France' in November 1658. Charles himself had been away for 11 years.

'Among (Charles's) acquired endowments these are the most eminent,' Tuke wrote. 'He understands Spanish and Italian, speaks and writes French correctly...he is a true friend to Literature and to Learned Men.

'It is possible that in the heat of his youth he may have rendered to the powerful charms of beauty, yet I am certain that for many years he hath been so chaste and cautious that I have not heard the least whisper of any indecent gallantry,' he adds.

At first, Charles put Tuke's diplomatic skills to use in missions to the French court. Then Tuke picked up the hint that Charles would like an English version of Calderon's play.

The 'prologue at court' mentioned earlier sets the story out thus:

'As to a dying Lamp, one drop of Oyl
Gives a new Blaze, and makes it live a while;
So th' Author seeing his decaying Light,

And therefore thinking to retire from sight,
Was hindered by a Ray from th'upper Sphere,
Just at that time he thought to disappear.'

One scholar, Martin Hume, took the 'dying lamp' idea too literally and wrote that 'Tuke was at this time elderly and had intended to live quietly in the country'. Tuke was actually in his mid-to-late forties and soon to embark on two marriages and the production of three children!

Tuke 'retired' only so long as it took to produce his translation and adaptation of the Spanish play. Fortunately, he knew just the quiet spot for such unaccustomed labour. His friend Henry Howard of Norfolk had a villa in large grounds at Aldbury, near Guildford.

Howard and his garden make several appearances in Evelyn's diary. Evelyn first met 'the Rt. Honorable Henry Howard' at Padua while on his grand tour in 1645. Ten years later he visited him at Aldbury, where Howard had 'begun to build and alter the gardens much'. By the time Tuke stayed with Howard seven years later the garden would have had time to mature.

Acknowledging his debt in a dedication to the play, Tuke wrote: 'Since it is your pleasure (noble sir) that I should hold my fortune from you; like those tenants who pay some inconsiderable trifle in lieu of a valuable rent, I humbly offer you this poem in acknowledgement of my tenure. I am well pleased with this occasion to publish my sense of your favours, since it seems to me a kind of ingratitude to be thankful in private. It was bred upon the terrace-walks in your garden at Aldbury; and, if I mistake not, it resembles the place where it was brought up: the plot is delightful, the elevations natural, the ascents easy, without any great embellishments of art.

'I designed the character of Antonio as a copy of your steady virtue; if it appear, to those who have the honour to know you, I take leave to inform them that you have not sat to me long.'

Perhaps this can be interpreted as Howard not distracting his guest from his literary labours. 'On the death of his first wife in 1662, Howard is said to have fallen into a deep melancholy,' says the DNB, so there would not have been too many days of chatter and evenings of drinking,

There is a portrait in the National Portrait Gallery painted around 1680, which may be of Howard, who by that date had become Duke of Norfolk. It is now 'possibly after Sir Peter Lely', but a century ago the DNB attributed it to Mary Beale (1633-99) the first truly professional female artist.

The roman-nosed, slightly moustached, heavily wigged gentleman who stares out of a heavy oval fruit-decorated surround gives us an idea of the man upon whom Tuke claimed to have based his hero Antonio. Regrettably, there seems to be no portrait of Tuke himself.

Back at court and with his play successfully staged and in print, Tuke soon went one better than his ancestor Sir Bryan, being both knighted and made a baronet. Whether he has a better claim than Sir Henry Irving to be the first recipient of a knighthood for services to the theatre cannot be established because there were no citations in 1663-4.

And whether his services also included further playwriting is also uncertain. When Tuke's publisher Henry Herringman brought out an English version of Corneille's *Pompee* in 1664 the title page merely stated that it had been 'translated out of French by certain persons of Honour'. The theatre historian Allardyce Nicoll gives the authors as Edmund Waller, Lord Burkehurst, Sir Charles Sedley, Edward Filmer, Sidney Godolphin 'and a few others'. Pepys, who attributed it to 'several noble persons, among other my Lord Burkehurst', read it on the way down river in June 1666, just before the trip on which he reread *The Adventures*. He found it 'but a mean play and the words and sense not very extraordinary'. If Tuke had any hand in it, it was perhaps a good thing it did not become widely known. And Tuke had denied any intention of further playwriting in his prologue to *The Adventures*. While he hoped 'to take all England with a Spanish plot', he was not concerned if it should suffer shipwreck like the Armada, 'For by the example of the King of Spain, He resolves ne'r to trouble you again.'

On the other hand, Henry Herringman knew a 'selling' author when he had one. In an advertisement printed at the end of an edition of Sir John Denham's poems in 1684, he offered, among other books, 'By Samuel Tuke and several persons of honour, *Pompey*'.

If Tuke stuck to his resolve to write no more plays after *The*

Adventures he was joining a very large group of 'one-play writers'. A list of 123 1660-1700 authors compiled by Allardyce Nicoll includes no less than 60 who are credited with one play, some of them 'unstaged' and only Tuke's achieving fame. Instead of seeking that elusive second success as a writer, Tuke was setting up in his new titles, as Sir Samuel Tuke, Knight, Baronet, of Cressing Temple in the County of Essex, with a coat of arms carrying three gold lions on a red and blue background.

Not a lot was known about the Tukes at Cressing except that they did not keep their family seat there long, until modern research into family documents held in Leicestershire Record Office sorted things out.

The Temple, once a preceptory of the Knights Templars, went to the Smyth/Neville family at the Reformation. They were royalists and when Henry Neville was 'taken in arms' in 1644 he was fined £6,000, with the alternative of forfeiting his estates. He raised the money, but had to take out two mortgages on Cressing Temple.

'In 1657, James Winstanley, Edward Sedgewick and George Tuke [Samuel's brother] entered into an agreement to purchase the property for £21,000. The timber was to be cut, the estate sold as soon as possible, the mortgages paid off and the profit or loss shared by the partners,' as is explained in a recent Essex Record Office publication on the history of Cressing Temple. 'George Tuke was to take up residence in the mansion in order to facilitate the selling of the property.'

George took to the mansion life in style, inviting friends to stay. John Evelyn records that he went with his wife to keep Christmas 1658 with cousin George. Samuel was in London and called on Evelyn in November 1658, but if he was in the party Evelyn doesn't say so.

With the Restoration, disposal of the property began. A shipchandler associate of Samuel Pepys bought the timber - 600 oak trees and 120 ash trees - all to be delivered ready sawn to Rotherhithe within five years. The mansion itself was unoccupied by 1662 and George Tuke was giving his address as Greenwich (where he is buried).

Even if he never went there, Cressing Temple still sounded a good address for Tuke to give as his 'family seat' when he was made baronet.

In June 1664, the new baronet was married to Mary Guldeford, 'kinswoman to my Lord Arundel of Wardour, by the Queen's Lord Almoner, L Aubigny, in St James's Chapel', as Evelyn recorded, adding that the couple 'solemnized the wedding night at my house with much company'. Four years later, his first wife having died in childbirth in Paris in 1666, he married Mary Sheldon, a dresser to Queen Catherine once again being bedded at Evelyn's house, 'many friends accompanying the bride'.

He was elected one of the first members of the Royal Society, for which he wrote a paper on 'the History of the Generation and Ordering of Green Oysters, commonly called Colchester oysters', a process carried out under the control of the Court of Admiralty.

Sprat's *History of the Royal Society*, published in 1667, gave this in full, explaining: 'The Royal Society has set about collecting Histories of Nature, Art or Works by the plainest method and from the plainest information. They have fetched their intelligence from the constant and unerring use of experienced men of the most unaffected and more unartificial kinds of life. The instances that I shall give of this their manner of collecting Histories shall be of Works that of Saltpetre, of Arts that of Dying, and of Nature that of Oysters, which last may perhaps seem a subject too mean to be particularly alleged, but to me appears worthy to be produced. For though the British oysters have been famous in the World ever since this island was discovered, yet the skill how to order them aright has been so little considered among ourselves that we see at this day it is confined to some few narrow creeks of one single county.'

Tuke, in the capacity of 'unaffected and unartificial man of experience', used his local knowledge of those creeks to distinguish between the colour of oysters at Tollesbury, near Layer Marney, and at Brightlingsea, on the Frating side of the Colne.

Pepys, describing an accidental meeting with Tuke at his booksellers in February 1669, said of him: 'I think a little conceited but a man of very fine discourse as any I have ever heard almost.'

In 1671, the continued success of *The Adventures* sent Tuke back to the text. In a preface to the third edition he claimed he began revising the play because he was 'desired by a Lady who has more than usual favour for this play (though in other things very Judicious) to make a song, and insert it where you may now read it; I found it...difficult to disobey the Commands of this *Excellent Person*.' No further clue is given as to who the lady might be. It is tempting to argue that it was the queen, Catherine of Braganza, who had Spanish blood on her mother's side. Tuke, who had served an earlier queen, was now associated with her household. Tuke explained that he had not cast his eyes on the play since it was first printed. He found some very obvious faults, which he blamed on 'being importuned by those for whose benefit this play was intended. I was even forced to expose it before it was fit to be seen.' The December 15 deadline still rankled nearly ten years later.

Despite taking much trouble in tidying up the text, Tuke hoped no-one would notice. 'If they who have formerly seen or read this play should not perceive the amendments, then I have touched the point, since the chiefest art in writing is the concealment of art,' he wrote.

Also in 1671 Samuel and the second Mary saw their son Charles christened at Somerset House 'by a popish priest with many odd ceremonies', as Evelyn reported. 'The godfathers were the King and Lord Arundel of Wardour and godmother the Countess of Huntingdon.' The couple also had two daughters.

Somerset House was the home of the queen. 'As Charles II did not find it compatible with his gallantries that his queen should be resident at Whitehall, he lodged her during part of his reign in this palace (Somerset House). This made it the resort of Roman Catholics,' as Brewer puts it in his *Survey of the Metropolis* 1816.

The year 1671 also saw the sale of Cressing Temple to the Lord Mayor of London, Sir Thomas Davies.

Tuke died on January 26 1674 and was buried in the vault of the chapel at Somerset House. The chapel, proposed in 1623 but not built until the 1630s, is described in *Inigo Jones' Complete Architectural Drawings*, by Harris and Higgott, as 'a deeply considered building, perhaps one of the most refined of any by Jones'. More importantly, it was one of the few licensed Roman Catholic chapels in the country at the time.

The chapel, along with the rest of the palace, fell into disrepair in the eighteenth century and was eventually demolished to make way for the present building. Any memorials in the chapel seem not to have been preserved.

It is one of those quirks of fortune that Tuke, whose fame while he lived depended upon his writing a smash hit play for the Lincoln's Inn Fields Theatre - converted from a tennis court - should be buried on the site of another tennis court. For this was the former use of the land chosen for Inigo Jones's chapel.

Sir Samuel was succeeded in his baronetcy by Charles, his only son, who went into the army, fighting and dying for James in Ireland in 1690. Since Charles had no heirs, the direct line and the title became extinct at the Battle of the Boyne.

3: ON STAGE AND IN PRINT

Samuel Pepys was not the only person who wanted to read *The Adventures*. The first edition, a small folio text, appeared within three months. Tuke's dedication to a future Duke of Norfolk was signed, but there was no author's name on the title page. It carried the date February 21 1662 (by the Julian Calendar in which 1663 did not start until March) and the words 'Imprimatur John Berkenhead'.

In this the author, his printer and publisher were following the Act Against Unlicensed and Scandalous Books and Pamphlets, 1649, renewed in 1652-3, under which all books should bear on their title page the printer's name and address and 'the Author's name, with his quality and place of Residence, or at least the Licenser's names where Licenses are required', (as the Annals of Printing, 1966, puts it).

At the Restoration, Sir Henry Herbert. who had first been appointed Master of the Revels in 1642, set about re-establishing his authority, but found that the times had 'given men new habits of reasoning, notions of privilege and properties of resistance', as the Victorian theatre historian Dutton Cook put it. 'Herbert applied to the courts of justice for redress but the verdicts of the judges were contradictory.'

Herbert seems to have often waived the requirement for plays to be read by his department before they were performed, provided theatre managers paid him his 40-shilling fee for a licence. But in early 1663 his deputy, Edward Hayward, was drafting a petition to the courts seeking to prove that 'the Master of the Revels hath not only the power of licensing all plays, poems and ballads, but of appointing them to the Press'. Whether he would succeed was uncertain.

Tuke, as a courtier anxious to keep in with the king and his officials, played safe and got the imprimatur. John Berkenhead had been a courtier since the days when Charles I held court in Oxford and on return from exile, had become an MP and a member of the Royal Society. In 1662-3 he was 'one of the masters of requests' and, presumably, an official in the Revels office.

A rumour that Samuel Tuke was not the author, or at least not the sole author, of *The Adventures*, began to circulate within two days of the play opening. On January 10 1663 Lady Anglesey wrote to her husband: 'Lord Bristol has made a play which was much commended.' The idea had a long life.

'It is worthy of note that the first edition of *The Adventures* bears no author's name,' says the DNB in its entry for George Digby, second Earl of Bristol.

'The Earl of Bristol's interest in Spanish drama suggests he may have provided a first draft,' says Allardyce Nicoll, in his *History of English Drama*. 'To be noted is the fact that on July 20 1664 Pepys had heard that it was by the same author as wrote *Worse and Worse*.'

What Pepys actually put in his diary was: 'After the lottery, I went to a play, only a piece of it, which was at the Duke's House. *Worse and Worse* - just the same manner of play and writ I believe by the same man as *The Adventures of Five Hours* - very pleasant it was.' This sounds more a judgement based on similarity of style than on something he heard. And it can be understood in the opposite way, as meaning that Tuke was the author of *Worse and Worse*.

Roscius Anglicanus in 1708 described *The Adventures* as 'wrote by the Earl of Bristol and Sir Samuel Tuke'. A footnote in the Society of Theatre Research reprint of Downes's book comments: 'Bristol did write Spanish romances but all other sources suggest that Tuke was the sole author of this play.' The writer seems not to have heard of Pepys's comment, and Downes was not just passing on Pepys's opinion, since the Diary was not translated from shorthand and printed until many years after Downes wrote his theatrical history.

The only 'Spanish romance' by Lord Bristol to survive, *Elvira*, was printed in 1667 as 'written by a person of quality'. When it appears alongside *The Adventures* in Dodsley's *Collection of Old Plays* in 1744 the compiler supplements this attribution with the words: '...which I am informed from very good hands was George Lord Digby, commonly called the great Lord Digby. Whether his merit as a poet is equal to his character as a statesman the reader must judge, but I thought a piece of this nature from so celebrated a man could not fail of being acceptable to the public.' By the 19th century Dodsley reprints were just saying 'by Lord Bristol'.

Besides *Elvira*, first recorded as acted at court in late 1663, he wrote *Worse and Worse*, which was acted at Lincoln's Inn Fields in 1664 and at court in 1666, and *Tis Better Than it Was*, but these two plays were never printed. Calderon plays with similar titles have been suggested as originals by the Society of Theatre Research and others, supporting the idea that the earl may have provided a literal translation of the Spanish original for Tuke to work from. This method has been much used in other periods of theatre history, when authors who have little Norwegian and less Russian rely upon such cribs to produce new acting versions of Ibsen and Chekhov.

Modern thinking has *Elvira* written in imitation of *The Adventures*, but with less success, being a very serious play where Tuke managed to lighten the tone.

Recent scholarship has also cleared up another confusion about the authorship of *The Adventures*. The strange idea that Samuel Tuke's brother George wrote the play can be traced to the Rev William Bray, who transcribed Evelyn's diary/memoir early in the nineteenth century. Clearly he struggled with the handwriting, particularly when it came to the two Tukes.

From the entry dated May 7 1656 he deciphered the information that 'in the afternoon I met Alderman Robinson to treat with Mr Papillion about the marriage of my cousin, George Tuke, with Mrs Fountain'. This gave him a name to start with. Then he found a 1660 'message from the king...by Colonel Tuke', with no christian name. Shortly afterwards he found 'Sir Samuel Tuke haranguing the house of Lords on behalf of the Roman Catholics'. Clearly another person altogether. Evelyn hadn't helped by giving Samuel his title four years before the king did so.

When Mr Bray got to the theatrical entries in December 1662 and January 1663 he found mentions of 'my kinsman' but also 'Sir'. Which Tuke was it? Bray settled for George. 'Sir George

Tuke' attended the December 23 rehearsal and 'my kinsman Sir George Tuke' the first night on January 8.

This version, republished in 1907 as an Everyman classic, was the best information available until 1955, by which time *The Adventures* had been the subject of three studies and numerous mentions in reference books. Allardyce Nicoll had pointed out 'the peculiar fact that Evelyn speaks of Sir George Tuke as the author'. Montague Summers, in his introduction to the 1927 English edition of the play, quotes Evelyn as saying 'I went with Sir George (Samuel) Tuke', which is playing it very safe. A.E.H. Swaen, introducing the Amsterdam edition of the same year, noted that 'Evelyn wrote George for Samuel'.

Then E.S. de Beer published what is now accepted as the authoritative edition of Evelyn's Diary. Mr de Beer transcribed the two diary entries both as 'S:' - neither George nor Samuel but a single, easily misread, initial.

If only writers could resist improving upon what they find in their sources...

Any doubts about the authorship should have been put at rest when a second edition of *The Adventures* appeared from the same publisher 12 months after the first.

This pocket edition, though printed on smaller pages, was from the first edition type. It remained unattributed on the title page, but verses were added in praise of the play and its author, written by people who were in no doubt that it was Samuel Tuke's work.

James Long testified to the success of Colonel Tuke's 'exemplary dramatic poem' in involving the audience:

'No more spectators now, we're actors all,
With every change our passions rise and fall.'

John Evelyn claimed kinship with the author of the 'incomparable play', forgetting the 'stiff and formal' comments he had committed to his diary and alleging:

'You in Five Hours have here performed more,
Than in Five Ages all our Bards before.'

Abraham Cowley dismissed any argument that Tuke's success was due to the Spanish original:

'You have not basely gotten it by stealth,
Nor by translation borrowed all its wealth,
But by a powerful spirit made it your own,
Metal before, money by you tis grown.'

Jasper Nedham put the case for the play in two lines:

'Good plot, clean language, well-weighed sense,
Challenge applause and make their own defence.'

And Lord Carlile, among several who urged the dramatist to continue his good work, declared:

'Teach us the Art to please your virtuous way,
For though our Vices have debauched the stage,
More poets made like you may stop that rage.'

An advertisement pasted on the back of the title page of the British Library copy reads: 'You may be furnished with most sorts of plays at the White Lion near Chancery Lane end in Fleet Street by Thomas Dring.' Play-reading was popular.

How many of the 'most sorts of plays' which Thomas Dring sold met the standard claimed for *The Adventures* is uncertain. The next long run on the London stage of the 1660s was *Henry VIII*, Fletcher and Shakespeare's play revived by Sir William Davenant, with the rich scenes then in fashion, and an elaborate setting of Katherine's vision, but not rewritten as he did *Macbeth*, *The Tempest* and *Measure for Measure*. The next big money-maker was George Etherege's *The Comical Revenge, or Love in a Tub*, which took £1000 in its first month at Lincoln's Inn Fields in 1664. It was part serious, written in heroic couplets, but with a strong comic underplot which launched the Restoration comedy of manners. Soon, there would be pure comedies and heroic tragedies, rather than the style Tuke called 'tragi-comedy'.

The 1664 edition of *The Adventures* coincided with the first of many public theatre revivals. The play remained popular at court also.

It was acted there by the Duke's Company on December 3 1666. Pepys, who had reread the play on the river that summer, didn't go, though he had been to *Love in a Tub* at court on October 29. Pepys could always ignore his own resolutions not to go to plays if there was a court performance he could get into.

In fact, he did not go to a public theatre between May 15 1665 and December 7 1666, mainly because of the plague and the fire, and feeling that he ought not to be seen at such frivolous amusements. This feeling survived 14 days after the theatre reopened in 1666, and when he did go to *The Maid's Tragedy* he muffled himself in a cloak 'in mighty pain lest I be seen by anybody to be at a play'.

Three years later, on January 27 1669, Pepys went 'to the Duke's Playhouse and there (for the third time) saw *The five hours adventures*, which hath not been acted a good while before but once, and is a most excellent play I must confess.'

So excellent that just over a fortnight later, on February 15, 'my wife and I went to Whitehall and there, by means of Mr Cooling (secretary to the Lord Chamberlain) did get into the play, the only one we have seen this winter (did he mean 'together' or 'at court'?). It was *The Five Hours Adventure* but I sat so far I could not hear well, nor was there any pretty woman that I did see but my wife. The house was very full.'

The play's continued popularity led to a 'third impression' (to yet another page size but the first time the type had been reset, so strictly it should have been called the 'second edition'). 'Revised and corrected by the author, Sir Samuel Tuke, Knight and Baronet', it was very different from the no-name title pages of the earlier editions.

The revised tragi-comedy is described as 'as it is acted at His Royal Highness the Duke of York's Theatre'. The 'is' makes clear this was not an author's vanity rewriting but a working text for a play with a continuing life on the stage.

The performances which coincided with its publication took place at Lincoln's Inn Fields Theatre. On April 20 1672 the play was 'performed before royalty' once again, but this time royalty came to the players instead of the other way round. This may have been because the play was now being staged at the newly-opened Dorset Gardens Theatre, designed by Christopher Wren and much more magnificent than any theatre London had previously seen. Drury Lane, the home of the King's Men, had burnt down in January 1672 so when *The Adventures* was revived it was the only play on offer to a London audience.

In the next century *The Adventures* continued to appear on the stage and in print, with editions in 1704 and 1712 and performances in 1707 (Haymarket) and 1727 (Drury Lane). By this time the play was being anthologised in Best English Plays and the *Select Collection of Old Plays* 'printed for R. Dodsley in Pall Mall' and published abroad (there was a Dutch edition in 1711).

Eighteenth century authors had no qualms about quarrying in old plays to produce works of their own, more suited to the times. Lord Bristol's *Elvira*, having vanished from the stage, was treated in this way. 'From some part of it Mrs Susannah Centlivre seems to have borrowed *A Wonder, or A Woman Keeps a Secret,*' says David Erskine Baker, editor of the *Biographica Dramatica*. It seems to have worked - her 1714 version was much acted and was chosen by David Garrick for his farewell performance as late as 1776.

It took longer for the fate of being rewritten for a new age to overtake *The Adventures*. In 1767, Thomas Hull, who also adapted *The Comedy of Errors* and *Timon of Athens* for the tastes of his age, rechristened *The Adventures* as *The Perplexities*. 'Only an alteration from *The Adventures of Five Hours* and, like most other comedies of Spanish origin, is a chaos of balconies, cloaks, rapiers and dark lanthornes,' opined Baker in 1782.

In his introduction, Hull confessed: 'The editor of this comedy thinks it his duty to declare that, in point of fable, he is entirely indebted to an old play written by Sir Samuel Tuke.'

However, if the plot met with Hull's favour, the language didn't. 'Finding, upon examination of the original, the language to consist entirely of measure and rhyme, a style by no means suited to the use of comedy, it appeared indispensibly necessary to new-write it.'

A footnote refers to 'this comedy (*The Perplexities*) having been treated with very distinguished marks of candour and encouragement in the representation'.

The 'new-writing' is in prose. Character names are adjusted Porcia and Camilla become Honoria and Felicia (Camilla had been Nise in the Spanish original, so this was not the first time a translator had seen fit to make such an adjustment). There are early references to the 'secret door' which links two houses, and to 'the present hour of seven', helping to explain how the action is managed and pointing to its being completed in the five hours of the original title,

Oddly enough, Hull's prose rewrite was published without his name on the title page. Like the early editions of *The Adventures*, its title pages bore a Latin tag from Horace.

The Perplexities ran for ten nights at Covent Garden, the final performance being by command of George III and Queen Charlotte, so that the rewrite shared royal patronage with its source play. London and Dublin editions of 1767 were not followed up by later publishers, but *The Adventures* was reprinted in Dodsley editions in 1780, 1825 and 1874, the last edited by W.C. Hazlitt.

A German translation appeared in 1866, and a three-act adaptation by Meyrick Milton was performed in Edinburgh and at the Strand Theatre, London, in 1893.

Having been attributed to Calderon by Tuke, a different author had come into favour by the beginning of the twentieth century, but not without a warning note being attached to the new attribution. Martin Hume, in *Spanish Influence on English Literature*, published in 1905, wrote that 'every authority and textbook says it is by Coello. Authorities and textbooks, however, have a somewhat misleading habit of copying each other on minor points without much investigation.'

When the two 1927 editions of Tuke's play appeared, the question of who wrote the Spanish original was pursued by both Summers and Professor Swaen.

Summers's title page describes the play as 'by Sir Samuel Tuke, adapted from the Spanish of an Unknown Play by Calderon'.

In his introduction, Summers rehearses the many debts of the English stage to the literature of Spain, beginning almost 50 years before the closure of the theatres by the Puritans in 1642. On the origins of this play, he describes *Los Empeños de Seis Horas* (The Complications of Six Hours) as 'certainly for a long time attributed to Calderon. It seems to have been written about 1641 or a few years later, and in that vast library of Spanish drama which from 1652 to 1714 was published under the general title *Comediea Nuevas de las Mejores Ingenios de España*, it appears under the name of Calderon, but it is not included in the various collections of that author's works, and it seems almost certain that it was written by Don Antonio Coello y Ochoa, although even this cannot be maintained without some slight qualification, but about the middle of the sixteenth (sic) century there was issued *La que Pasa en una Noche (What Happens in one Night)*, comedia famosa de Don Antonio Coello. This is practically the same play as *Los Empeños de Seis Horas*, which was printed in Madrid in 1657 and attributed to Calderon in the eighth volume of *Comedias Nuevas* we have mentioned above, but Calderon definitely declared that the comedy was not his work, and Don Emilio Cotarelo, the distinguished Spanish scholar, in his *Life of Coello*, says that possibly neither is it to be attributed to this dramatist...In fact the play so much resembles Calderon that it has been suggested it may be by some close and not unskilful imitator of that great master.'

So a distinguished Spanish scholar cannot decide upon its original authorship. Summers supplies a potted biography of Coello (born Madrid 1611, poet, praised by Lope de Vega, said to have helped Philip IV compose a play about the Earl of Essex 'but it is certain that the King had no hand in this drama', knighted, died 1642) and ends: 'he does not appear even to have seen his plays through the press, and with regard to their fate his attitude was that of real or feigned indifference.'

Perhaps this encouraged Summers to stick with the traditional attribution of *The Adventures* to Calderon.

Summers was writing an introduction to an edition for which B. van Thal collated the third and fourth editions of Tuke's play. Professor Swaen, at Amsterdam University, reprinted and compared the first and third editions of the play and *Los Empeños de Seis Horas* in the original Spanish. The text, dated 1657, bears Calderon's name. I have suggested above that it was probably the edition which King Charles read. It may also be presumed to be the edition Tuke used. Someone has written 'Coello' in pen on the title page which Swaen reproduces, and Swaen plumps for Coello as the author. The play is 'now credited to Coello' in David Womersley's *Restoration Drama* (Blackwell, 2000), which reprints the first edition text of *The Adventures*. Womersley does not have room in his short introduction to the play to look at the arguments.

4: THE CRITICAL RECEPTION

More important, perhaps, than who wrote the Spanish original is whether Tuke merely translated it or adapted it in ways which made it significantly his play, and how far it is worth consideration in its own right.

Leading the field for critical comment was John Dryden. His first play, the comedy *The Wild Gallant,* was staged a month after *The Adventures* and seen by both diarists. Evelyn merely notes date (February 5, 1663), place (the Great Hall) and title. Pepys, who saw it on February 23 1663 'at court', was as unhappy about it as he was delighted with *The Adventures.* It was 'ill acted, so poor a thing as I never saw in my life almost. The King did not seem pleased at all,' he wrote.

The most interesting thing about *The Wild Gallant* from the point of view of this study is that Dryden sought to pre-empt unflattering comparison with Tuke's comedy. In an opening scene, two astrologers are asked to estimate the likelihood of his play being a success. They go through the zodiac as it would be on February 5, meeting various hazards:

'But yet the greatest mischief does remain,
The twelfth Apartment bears the Lord of Spain,
Whence it concludes it is your author's lot
To be indangered by a Spanish plot.'
'Our play is English and the growth your own,
As such it yields to English Plays alone,'

Dryden declares through his Prologue.

The excuse for failure was needed. Dryden, publishing a revised edition six years later, declared: 'It would be a great impudence in me to say much of a Comedy which has had but indifferent success in the action. I made the Town my Judges and the greater part condemned it.' But he pointed out: 'Yet it was received at Court and was more than once the Divertisement of His Majesty by his own command.' Perhaps when Pepys attended the second command performance, Charles was regetting having asked to see the comedy again.

In his *Essay on Dramatic Poesy* (1668) Dryden uses Tuke's play as his example in a discussion about the mixing of serious and comic material derived from the Spanish by Moliere and others.

'There is scarce one of them without a veil and a trusty Diego who drolls much after the rate of the *Adventures*. But their humours - if I may grace them with that name - are so thin sown that never above one of them comes up in any play. I dare take upon me to find more variety of them in some one play of Ben Jonson than in all theirs together.'

The acid tone is carried on into a discussion of Jonson's *The Silent Woman*, describing how 'its action is limited to three hours and a half, which is no more than is required for the presentment on the stage - a beauty perhaps not much observed; if it had, we should not have looked on the Spanish translation of *Five Hours* with so much wonder.'

But elsewhere he offers a clue as to why, despite any thinness of its comedy and unoriginality in its timing, *The Adventures* succeeded.

'I grant that the French have performed what was possible on the groundwork of the Spanish plays. What was pleasant before they have made regular. But there is not above one good play to be writ upon all these plots. They are too much alike to please often, which we need not the experience of our own stage to justify.'

Tuke wrote (for English audiences, at any rate) the 'one good play' which, by coming first into the field, triumphed where copies failed.

One of the most favourable mentions in critical literature occurs (improbably) in Laurence Echard's introduction to his 1698 translation of the plays of Terence. He gives *The Adventures* as his example of a play which observes the unity of time, with Jonson's *The Silent Woman* as a play which observes both time and action (only one story, no sub-plots), and Dryden's *All For Love* as a play which also observes the unity of place - one setting.

Not bad company for Tuke's play to be seen in! But Echard goes further, straying well away from Terence to describe *The Adventures* as 'one of the pleasantest stories that ever appeared upon our stage, and has as much variety of plots and intrigues, without anything being precipitated, improper, or unnatural as to the main action.'

Martin Hume, in *Spanish Influence on English Literature* (1905), represents the other end of the scale. He writes: 'Before the indirect adaptation of Spanish intrigue through the French had become the fashion under Charles II - for it took some time for Dryden and his followers to get to work and hit the taste of the court and public - a direct adaptation from the Spanish was made of one play, which attained a success, as it seems to us, out of all proportion to its merits.

'But however that may be, it was practically a reintroduction to the eager English public of the Spanish comedy of intrigue which, from that day to this, has never left the English stage: the comedy of contrary purposes, of mistaken personalities, and of mixed up lovers, ultimately sorted out to everyone's satisfaction.

'Pepys and other perhaps more competent critics pronounced the play to be the best specimen of the comedy of intrigue that had ever been seen in England. Reading it now the play seems not much better, if no worse than, dozens of Lope's and Calderon's plays, and far behind the best of them; but the London public at the time were unjaded, perhaps uncritical, and the play was accepted as a work of genius.'

Some ten years after Hume, Allison Gaw, head of English at the University of Southern California, set about turning her thesis on *Sir Samuel Tuke's Adventures of Five Hours in relation to the 'Spanish Plot' and to Dryden* into an introduction to a reprint of the first edition of the play. In this she was unsuccessful, but the introduction on its own did get into print, from the Waverly Press of the University of Pennsylvania, in 1917.

Gaw notes how Tuke makes the hero far more the heroic ideal than Coello, and that Tuke's Camilla is also more heroic – stabbing her would-be rapist with his own dagger is not in the Spanish.

She also compares the 1663 and 1671 editions. Dryden had criticised Tuke for writing lines which met the requirements of the verse at the cost of putting the words in an order no-one would have used in everyday speech. Gaw finds 30 such lines rectified in the 1671 edition. There were also some 333 entirely new lines, half of them in rhymed couplets.

She concluded that Tuke had not been revising for a new taste so much as 'to give a final polish to the work on which chiefly rested his claim to a place in the world of letters'.

But as her title suggests, Gaw was principally concerned to explore the effect of *The Adventures* on later plays. She mentions Lord Bristol's three dramas, but argues against Dryden taking from Spanish sources; finds Wycherley's plays more influenced by Moliere; and decides that the direct influence of Spain, minimal as it was, lasted only for ten years or so.

'It is a striking fact that in the 30 years after 1672 the only English play known to have been founded upon a Spanish drama is Crowne's *Sir Courtly Nice*, 1685, which was made not spontaneously but by direct request of the King.'

Swaen mentions not having had the chance of reading Gaw, but quotes Hume's dismissive comments on Tuke's play. He does not allow them to put him off the task of rehabilitating it.

'The renewed interest in the drama of the Restoration has given me the courage to edit Tuke's play which, in its two forms and from the fact that it is based on a Spanish original, is of no slight importance in the history of English dramatic literature in the seventeenth century,' he begins.

He sums up as follows: 'a typical play...the plot is intricate, so hopelessly so that one wonders how the actors could perform it without losing their way in the labyrinth. There are mistaken identities, veiled ladies, extinguished lights; the wrong houses and the wrong apartments once entered, swords are drawn; confusion is worse confounded by a stupid servant; an irascible father (sic) rants about honour. But the knot is dextrously untangled and at the conclusion all seems so simple and the reader is so neatly landed where he expected to land that he feels inclined to bow to the spirit of the author and exclaim "well done".'

Swaen compares the Spanish and English versions thus: 'The (Coello) piece is mainly spectacular. The heart and the mind are hardly satisfied, and there lies the difference between the Spanish original and the English adaptation.

'The thing which strikes us is the didactic tone of Tuke's play. In the Spanish piece, there is a good deal of talk about love and honour but there are few sententious sayings which are numerous in the English play. The result is that although the plot is Spanish the dramatis personae are no longer Spanish, they are anglicised Spaniards. The conversation is more natural and vivid, the development of the plot clearer.'

Montague Summers notes a 17th century reference by Gerald Langbaine to the play's being 'one of the best new plays now extant for economy and contrivance', adding: 'It has, of course, been remarked that Sir Samuel has managed to reduce the Six Hours of the Spanish author to Five.'

His own summing up of the play and justification for its being reprinted is as follows: '*The Adventures of Five Hours* is a very important, a very interesting, and, I think we may truly claim, a very excellent drama. It is remarkable for its lofty ideals and the purity, ay, the nobility of its language.

'Surely it is not insignificant that a Restoration audience who are often crassly condemned as if their one itch and joy was ever to listen to bawdy jests and lickerish repartee should have received Tuke's scenes with enthusiasm and delight; surely it is not unimportant to remember that so clean and continent a play achieved a run of unprecedented length, a veritable triumph which passed into a tradition of the stage.

'It should be noticed that Tuke often employs rhyme, and this form, together with his exalted theme of love and honour, certainly foreshadow the heroic play with peculiar distinction. Indeed the debt of the heroic drama to the sentiments and qualities of the Spanish theatre has never yet been fully recognised nor appreciated. Tuke's complete mastery of his technique is for the author of a single play amazing in its sureness and dexterity, nor is his skill altogether due to the Spanish original, although of course *Los Empaños* stood him in unfailing service throughout.

'Very agreeably does the light gossip of the servants over their chocolate - and each, the butler, the usher, the groom, is cleverly individualized - relieve the graver scenes of Castilian dignity and pride, nor are the humours of honest Diego unamusing. In fact, the laughter is admirably managed, nor is the jest preserved too long.

'The serious intrigue at times appears to be so entangled that we are well-nigh afraid it cannot be unravelled without some violent snap or jar, and yet the author patiently and perseveringly weaves the perfect pattern of his play with the utmost simplicity and the utmost naturalness to its very end.

'Perhaps we can pay Sir Samuel Tuke no more generous compliment and no greater meed of praise than by expressing our keen regret that he did not enrich the English theatre with many other comedies equally combining the high ideals and superlative craftsmanship of this admired drama.'

Fifty years on from Summers and Swaen and seventy after Martin Hume, another scholar with the same surname, Robert D. Hume, put *The Adventures* under scrutiny for his book *The Development of English Drama in the Late Seventeenth Century*.

Hume read all 500 or so surviving plays of the period, but picked only eight for detailed consideration, beginning with Tuke's play. His commentary is the only one recommended for 'further reading' about *The Adventures* in Womersley's Restoration Drama anthology.

Hume arranges his eight plays 'in a rough order of descending seriousness, from exemplary romance to farce'. He notes the 'tragi-comedy' designation by Tuke and the tendencies towards heroic drama, but also the domestic setting and concerns, the amusing servants, the lack of rant, and the romantic-comedy structure with a double wedding in prospect at the end. He points out that Diego became a byword for a comic servant, turning up in a Dryden play, and drawing laughs right through the play.

His summing up finds 'purity, psychological acuity, humour, exemplary method and sustained tension'.

But Hume also quotes Pepys's 'customary exuberant superlatives' about the play at its premiere, and notes that 'praise of the unities and moral purity has perhaps seemed uninviting to recent critics'. And he cannot ignore Pepys's later comment, with which this account of *The Adventures* began.

'Worse yet, on 20 August 1666 Pepys notes that he was reading *Othello*, "which I ever heretofore esteemed a mighty good play; but having so lately read *The Adventures of Five Hours* it seems a mean thing". This curious judgement has both damaged Pepys's credit as a critic and left scholars wary of Tuke's play.'

I hope I have shown that Pepys (though expressing a heterodox opinion) was not indulging in 'customary exuberances' but justifying to himself, in his private diary, why he felt drawn back and back to Tuke's play, when there were other 'mighty good' ones he could have turned to.

The point about damaging *The Adventures* is a serious one. 'Among modern scholars only Summers voices more than tepid approval,' Hume reports, quoting Summers's verdict on it as 'a very important, interesting, excellent play'.

'I concur, and cannot imagine how the work acquired its reputation for deadly dullness. Not only is the piece of great significance historically, but it is thoroughly entertaining.'

Hume's very detailed analysis of the theatre of the late seventeenth century, and the critical responses to them down the years, comes again and again to the point that many of the plays are unsuited for reading, much less critical study, being never intended for either, but that they are, nevertheless, 'highly effective theatrical vehicles'.

'Perhaps just a delicious joke' is how he sums up Congreve's *Love for Love*, one of the acknowledged masterpieces of Restoration drama.

Hume even has his own version of Pepys's *Othello* judgement: 'I would rather see a spirited production of (Thomas Ravenscroft's) *The Citizen Turned Gentleman* than any performance imaginable of (William Wycherley's) *The Gentleman Dancing Master.*'

Both plays were written in 1672. One author is in the 'canon', the other decidedly not - though the Royal National Theatre set about putting this right with a production of Ravenscroft's *The London Cuckolds* in 2001.

This is, of course, the real test, to which so few of Hume's 500 plays have been put in living memory - a test long overdue for *The Adventures of Five Hours*.

STAGING THE PLAY

Enough has been said about the merits, or otherwise of Tuke's play. It is time for a summary of the plot, suggestions on how the play may have been staged in 1663, and some thoughts about how it could be tackled in the twenty-first century.

For the 'incomparable plot', Tuke relies upon his Spanish author, but many of the details are his own. Unlike Dryden, Wycherley and others who followed him, he sticks to a Spanish setting - two adjoining houses in Seville, plus the garden of one of them, the street outside and another house only a street or two away.

The inhabitants include the choleric, jealous and revengeful Don Henrique and his well-natured moral friend Don Carlos - the descriptions are from the extended dramatis personae Tuke wrote for his third revised edition. Both men have sisters of a dangerous age, for whom they must find husbands. For Porcia, Henrique has arranged a proxy contract with an army officer. Don Carlos disapproves and would never do such a thing for Camilla.

It is no surprise that Porcia already has a lover, Don Octavio, who has been wooing her at Camilla's house. But she cannot tell her brother so because Octavio has killed, in self defence, a friend of Henrique, and is currently in hiding.

If Porcia thinks a lover she cannot name, plus the threat of an arranged marriage, are bad, Camilla thinks her situation is worse. She 'loves one who she shall never see' – an army officer who rescued her from rape during a battle but was then separated from her before she could give him her name. She knows that he was called Don Antonio. He is, of course, the army officer who (despairing of ever seeing again the unknown woman he rescued) has now agreed to be contracted by proxy to Porcia.

Antonio arrives in Seville, twitted by his servant Sancho, who cannot decide which is the better joke - Antonio having 'fallen in love with one you hardly saw', or 'marrying one you never saw'. The first person he meets is Octavio, 'my comrade when I first bore arms', and they share their news, military and romantic, though without spelling out all the details.

When Antonio catches his first glimpse of 'Porcia' it is actually Camilla, because the real Porcia has seized an opportunity to slip away with Octavio. What luck! His proxy bride is 'her who's always present to my thoughts'. He goes into raptures to Henrique, who knows Porcia is missing and thinks he is being mocked.

Henrique is after Octavio's blood and Antonio offers his sword in support, but when he realises that Octavio is his old comrade he has to switch sides. Then Antonio recalls the love he bears to 'Porcia' and calls upon Octavio to renounce her. Never! So the 'rivals' do battle, until Henrique arrives...

'There's some mystery in this,' says Carlos, to deaf ears.

At last the two 'Porcias', and whom they are to pair off with, are sorted out, to the satisfaction of everyone except Henrique, who wants to consult his honour.

'You cannot take a better counsellor than your sister's honour,' says Carlos sensibly.

This outline omits a great many of the complications. Interrupted conversations, garden walls that have to be climbed, a sedan chair which half the cast believe contains Porcia being taken home and the rest know contains Octavio making his escape, and a lot of locked doors - plus the fact that virtually the whole play takes place at night - stop the truth emerging too soon.

The honour code is used to motivate characters and move the plot, but gently mocked.

There are diversions into discussion of the war news. The original Spanish play was topical to the date of composition, 1632, with a very long speech indeed for Antonio in which he reports on the recent fighting at Maastricht (history) as well as on his meeting with the unknown woman in peril (fiction). Tuke puts the play back a century for his history, but has lines which are topical to 1663.

A scene for the servants, containing rude comments on the Dutch, is all his own work, and designed to appeal to both the

general audience, at a time when war with Holland was immi-
nent, and to Charles, who had good reason to dislike the Dutch
after experiences with them during his exile.

A discussion between Octavio and Antonio about the recompense they expect for their long exile is also Tuke's and also
aimed, it must be assumed, at Charles.

Tuke, not his source, was responsible for the comedy in
Octavio's less than heroic follower Diego, who watches a street
battle from up a tree, and for Diego's romance with Porcia's
maid Flora. When it comes to the happy ending, they are not left
out of the knot-tying.

The way this is handled places the previous adventures where
they have really occurred, on a stage:

> Flo: Had ever such disorders a rare come-off?
> Methinks twould make a fine plot for a play.
> Die: Faith Flora, I would have the worst of that,
> For by the laws of comedy, twould be
> My lot to marry you.
> Ant: Thus ends the strange adventures of five hours...

The general setting of *The Adventures* is Seville, pronounced
with the emphasis on the first syllable. Tuke indicates the specif-
ic settings for each scene with phrases such as 'The Scene
Changes to a Garden'. But just how these changes were managed
at the Lincoln's Inn Fields Theatre is not always easy to work
out.

The theatre was a converted real tennis court, some 75 feet by
30 feet in size, plus two projecting wings, one lived in by
Davenant and the other converted into a scene dock.

Roughly half the length of the main room was occupied by
seating, with pit benches surrounded by boxes and a gallery. The
other half had a forestage, flanked by two pairs of proscenium
doors used for entrances, and a scenic stage behind. Most of the
action would have taken place on the forestage, where the light
was stronger and the actors were best placed to control the sometimes noisy audiences. But actors could move upstage, using
additional exits through the wings (see frontispiece).

One of the few clues to scenic methods available in theatres of the
period is a ground plan for Davenant's *The Siege of Rhodes* when it

was staged privately in 1656. An extended version of this opera was the opening show at Lincoln's Inn Fields. The diagram shows three sets of grooves at the back of the scenic stage: in which shutters representing different scenes could be slid in from each side.

It is a reasonable assumption that this style of setting (first developed by Inigo Jones for court masques before the civil war), would be brought for the first time into a public playhouse at Lincoln's Inn Fields.

Richard Southern, in his comprehensive account of scene-changing from Inigo Jones to Henry Irving, *Changeable Scenery*, lamented that for the Restoration period 'direct contemporary statements about the details and arrangement of scenery and about the machinery by which it worked are so few as to be non-existent. We have to fall back on implications. Restoration plays teem with suggestive stage-directions (but) these...are rarely directly explanatory.'

He finds help in Dryden's *The Wild Gallant*, including the key phrase 'the scene opens' as justification for believing that slidable scenery in grooves was used. But for his detailed examination of a complete play he turns to *The Adventures*. No less than ten pages are devoted to working out the conventions of the 1660s theatre from clues given in Tuke's stage directions.

Act one is described as 'Don Henrique's house', and the text makes plain this is an interior. Act two, 'The City of Sevil', is equally clearly a street scene, revealed perhaps by drawing back shutters which have depicted an interior. Then Southern notes that act three is also described as 'Don Henrique's House', though it takes place outside it, not inside.

'What happens in the next six pages is extremely puzzling,' Southern confesses. He tries to make sense of some complicated action by allocating the four doors facing into the forestage to various locations mentioned in the text. But he finds that he still needs another entrance, a fifth door.

This is at the moment when two separate parties are converging in supposed darkness upon a 'garden gate', which it seems cannot be any of the doors on either side of the forestage. Southern suggests that one set of grooves contained a garden wall, with a working gate and a climbable tree, which was slid into view for the first part of act three. This seems convincing, but what follows?

The next stage direction is 'The Scene changes to a garden, out of which they issue fighting'. Southern visualises the wall sliding away again, to reveal the continuing action. But this could be tricky, since Diego is still hiding in the tree at the time! It would be easier just for the gate to reopen, allowing the fighters to spill out of the garden into the street, whatever Tuke's scene-change note suggests.

Two more quick changes of scene follow, to 'The City of Sevil' and, only five lines later, to (inside) 'Don Henrique's House', with a few lines of linking dialogue by characters in a balcony over one of the proscenium doors. Overlooking street or garden, he wonders?

'To approach this long passage of stage-management with the preconception of our modern usage would involve difficulties of setting that would be insoluble without cutting or rearranging the script,' Southern decided in 1952. 'The implication seems unavoidable that this stage and this scenery were used somewhat differently from our modern way.'

'Modern usage' has since become much more flexible, with less emphasis on illusionistic sets. I suspect modern audiences would be happy to accept that indoors and outdoors can succeed one another on the same bare stage.

It is worth recalling that Restoration theatre proscenium doors were furnished with knockers and locks, so could stand equally well for a street door or an interior door. A good example of their use for both purposes occurs at the beginning of act five. A group of characters enter 'groaping as i'the dark' - a great deal of this play takes place at night but the theatre would, of course, be fully lit. They accompany a sedan chair and deliver its passenger Octavio to one door, through which he enters Don Carlos's house. So we start in the street, where the chair would be. As the chair is carried off, Octavio re-enters via the adjacent door, and we are now inside the house. With this flexibility accepted as a convention, it becomes much easier to see how the play can be done.

Four doors, sliding scenery in three sets of grooves and a little 'working on the audiences's imaginary powers' would do the trick. Whatever scenic arrangements were made, the vast bulk of the play would continue in an unlocalised space between the four doors.

The chances are that the scenery would not have looked particularly Spanish. No prompt book for *The Adventures* had come to light when several others for Lincoln's Inn Fields productions were reproduced in *Restoration Promptbooks* by Edward A Langhans (South Illinois University Press, 1981). They show that stock scenes were used from play to play, sometimes identified by the play for which they were first painted, at other times by phrases like 'The new Hall', a phrase describing a set prepared for *The Villain* in October 1662 and which was perhaps re-used for interior scenes in *The Adventures* three months later. *The Witty Faire One* is shown as being staged with three sets - garden, chamber and town - the chamber set serving for more than one location, as it could well be in *The Adventures*.

Marginal notes in these prompt copies show scene changes not given in the printed text, and it is reasonable to suppose that the actual staging of *The Adventures* did not follow exactly the descriptions supplied for readers of the first edition and which Tuke did not change when he revised the text for the third edition.

Southern notes, in his analysis of the 1661 staging of *The Siege of Rhodes*, that Davenant 'did not introduce scenery as an illusionistic setting but as a sort of counterpoint to the exposition of the plot'. So perhaps Tuke was reporting accurately what he had seen on the stage, and the absence or apparent misplacing of scene changes was deliberate? I suspect we will never know.

Modern theatres and ideas on staging vary so enormously that it is difficult to suggest how a director might approach the play if a Restoration-style production is not aimed at. However, a few of the problems which the play presents are worth discussing in general terms.

How Samuel Tuke wanted his play to be acted is made clear in the 1671 edition, where he expanded his original Dramatis Personae, providing the reader with 'the several Characters of the most Eminent Persons in the Play, that being acquainted with them at his first setting out, he may the better judge how they are carried on in the whole Composition; for Plays being Moral Pictures, their chiefest perfections consist in the Force and Congruity of Passions and Humours, which are the Features and Complexions of our Minds. And I cannot but hope that he will approve the Ingenuity of this Design, though possibly he may dislike the Painting.'

Tuke's list of 'persons' and 'characters' is given in full facing the first page of the play text. The character sketches are a great help to both actors and director. That Don Henrique is 'choleric, jealous, revengeful', while his sparring partner Don Carlos is 'a well-natured moral gentleman' gives a clear 'steer' to the performers but also points up the contrast between the two men which must be brought out if their scenes are to have variety and interest. Likewise, Porcia and Camilla are helped to avoid becoming too alike by Tuke's hints. Porcia is 'ingenious', the plotter, perhaps the more lively of the pair: Camilla is 'susceptible to love', asking for a softer performance, perhaps. But Porcia's ingenuities do not stop her being 'severely virtuous', and Camilla's susceptibility to love has to be balanced by cautiousness as to her honour. Bringing out the individual characteristics while also maintaining this overall tone is a pretty problem for the performers.

Tuke's explanations of 'who loves who' would, I feel, be a great help to actors starting work on the play. I have quoted in an earlier chapter commentators' wonder at how the actors found their way through the plot!

These explanations give away no secrets as to how 'it all comes out in the end'. Printed in full in a programme they would be a great help to audiences and in no way spoil enjoyment.

It is, to my mind, a distinct merit of the play that it gives a chance to shine to at least eight actors, rather than depending on one or two stars. Thomas Betterton, the actor who led the company, played Don Henrique. It is worth remembering that Henrique is not the stock 'heavy father'. He is Porcia's brother. All the main male roles are youngish (Betterton was 28 when he first acted Henrique). Henry Harris, who was thought better than Betterton by some who saw the two men act together, played Octavio (the character Tuke thought most highly of, if his dedicatory lines to Henry Howard are any guide). Mary Betterton played Porcia. Despite the play's success and many revivals, Henrique is not mentioned in lists of Betterton's acting triumphs, not, I suggest, because it is not a strong part but because the play is an ensemble piece, not a vehicle for one or two actors.

The play's *Five Hours* title suggests that it is very long (though not as long as in the original Spanish, when it was called *Six Hours*). There are about 3500 lines of dialogue, or more than three hours of speech, not allowing for time taken by stage business. If the play is not to outstay its welcome, it might be sensible to cut enough to keep it down to not more than three hours' playing time.

There is no detachable sub-plot and the 'comic relief' from Diego and Flora is very welcome. On the other hand an obvious cut is the song, which was added for the third edition. For any director who decides to do this, the end of act one in the first edition is printed as an alternative.

The servants' discussion of the war in Flanders, after Porcia and Camilla leave the stage in act one, can be made amusing, and the performers of the servant roles would be very sorry to see their best moments go! If, nevertheless, this is cut, Tuke provides a scene for Henrique, Ernesto and Silvio which is just long enough for the audience to believe that the girls have had time to tell each other the second halves of their stories before returning to the stage to lament their fates.

Better, I suggest, would be to set about trimming the longer speeches, taking out lines where a point seems to be being laboured, and carefully shortening scenes in which characters report to each other events the audience already know about.

Deleting whole sections of the play is fraught with danger, on the other hand. The carefully woven plot could fall apart.

The play need not depend upon wings and sliding shutters for its settings. While it could be given the full treatment in a theatre equipped with flying facilities or a revolve, it would, I believe be equally effective when played in a single setting, suggesting a Spanish town square, perhaps. This would need to provide several entrances (including that garden gate). An upper level would be a help, though in extremis a window at stage level could be used for balcony scenes, and anything strong enough to bear his weight for Diego's tree! To suggest interiors, more use could be made of chairs than seems to have been the fashion in 1663, when only the audience for the song were allowed to sit down! One table is the only other furniture mentioned in the stage directions.

An open stage version or production in the round, allowing actors to make entrances through the audience, would get close to the intimacy which must have been felt at Lincoln's Inn Fields. It would encourage direct contact with audience via the many asides. Don Henrique's opening soliloquy, in which the performer looks the gallants in the pit in the eye and laments the temper-controlling problems of 'we the unhappy men of fire' could be used to establish this contact from the 'off'.

On the plotting of entrances, my advice is to start with act five and work backwards, since the action gets steadily more complicated as the play proceeds, and any decisions as to which location each door leads to, if based upon the first two acts, will inevitably create problems later on! Essential properties are limited to swords and a sedan chair. (Octavio hiding his face behind Porcia's fan and walking between two poles carried by the 'chair-men' would do in the simplest staging). Flora's relighting candle seems more difficult, but full-size versions of this 'trick' can be bought from magic shops. Small ones are sold in the cake decorating section of your local supermarket, to tease children who are told to 'blow out the candles'!

As to costume, full Spanish (or Charles the Second) outfits, wigs and the rest would lift the play, provided the actors wear them casually and are not weighed down by them. 'Timeless with Spanish trimmings' would serve.

If contemporary dress is contemplated (and some Restoration play productions of recent years have attempted this) it is worth remembering the two main elements of the plot. The play revolves around an arranged marriage to a total stranger, and it is 'honour' that (however mocked) drives much of the action. A production set in today's 'society' would be hard to make credible, though an audience might accept one set in a (British) Asian community or among (American) Hispanic families.

The text which follows is based upon Tuke's revised and corrected edition of 1671, collated with the edition of 1712, from which some alternative readings have been adopted.

Speech headings have been regularised. Spelling has been modernised. Minor modifications have been made to abbreviations and other word-forms which could trip up a reader or actor.

But the great majority of Tuke's capital letters and commas have been preserved. Although at first glance there are far too many of them, they can be helpful in phrasing and placing emphasis, when speaking Tuke's verse.

SOURCES QUOTED IN THIS INTRODUCTION

ADAMS, Joseph Quincey. Dramatic Records of Sir Henry Herbert. Cornell University, 1917

BAKER, David Erskine (editor). Biographica Dramatica. London, 1782

BERRY, W & POOLE, E. Annals of Printing. Blandford Press, 1966

BOSWELL, Eleanore. Restoration Court Stage. Allen & Unwin, 1966

BREWER, J. Norris. Survey of the Metropolis. Wilson, 1816

BRISTOL, Lord. Elvira. Dodsley, 1744

BURKE, J. Baronetage. London, 1844

COOK, Dutton. The Book of the Play. Sampson Low, 1876

CORNEILLE, Pierre. Pompey (tr. Waller, etc). Herringman, 1664

DAVENANT, Sir William. The Works. London, 1673

DE BEER, E.S. The Tuke Family Tree. Notes and Queries, 1931

DENHAM, Sir John. Poems. Herringman, 1684

DOWNES, John. Roscius Anglicanus. Playford, 1708 (Society for Theatre Research reprint, 1987)

DRYDEN, John. Essay on Dramatic Poesy. London, 1668

DRYDEN, John. The Wild Gallant. Herringman, 1679

ECHARD, Laurence. Terence's Comedies Made English. London, 1698

EVELYN, John. Diaries. Edited by William Bray. Everyman, 1907

EVELYN, John. Diaries. Edited by E.S. de Beer. Oxford, 1959

FOSTER, Joseph (editor). Register of Grays Inn

GAW, Allison. Sir Samuel Tuke's Adventures of Five Hours in relation to the 'Spanish Plot' and to Dryden. University of Pennsylvania, 1917

GILDON, Charles. Life of Thomas Betterton. London, 1710

GUYVER, Robert M. Cressing Temple from Pre-History to the Present. Essex Record Office, 1991

HARRIS, J and HIGGOTT, F. Inigo Jones's Complete Architectural Drawings. Royal Academy of Art, 1989

HARTNOLL, Phyllis (editor). Companion to the Theatre. Oxford, 1957

HULL, Thomas. The Perplexities. London and Dublin, 1767

HUME, Martin. Spanish Influence on English Literature. Eveleigh Nash, 1905

HUME, Robert D. The Development of English Drama in the Late Seventeenth Century. Clarendon Press, 1976

LANGBAINE, Gerald. An Account of the English Dramatic Poets. 1691 (Hildesheim, 1968 reprint)

LANGHANS, Edward A. Restoration Promptbooks. South Illinois University Press, 1981

LENHEP, William J. (editor). The London Stage. South Illinois University Press, 1965

MORANT, Philip. History and Antiquities of the County of Essex. E.P. Publishing reprint, 1967

NICOLL, Allardyce. History of English Drama. Harrop, 1952

NICOLL, Allardyce. Restoration Drama, 1660-1700. Cambridge University Press, 1967

PEPYS, Samuel. Diaries, Edited by R. Latham and W. Matthews. Harper Collins, 1995

SOUTHERN, Richard. Changeable Scenery. Faber and Faber, 1952

SUMMERS, Montague. The Playhouse of Pepys. Routledge, 1935

SUMMERS, Montague. Restoration Theatre. Routledge, 1934

TUKE, Samuel. Character of Charles the Second by an Impartial Hand. London, 1660

TUKE, Samuel. History of the Generation and Ordering of Green Oysters. In Spratt, Thomas, History of the Royal Society. London, 1667

TUKE, Samuel. The Adventures of Five Hours. Herringman, 1663, 1664, 1671; Johnson, 1712; Dodsley, 1744; with introduction by Montague Summers, Holden, 1927; with introduction by A.E.H. Swaen, Amsterdam, 1927; with introduction by David Womersley, Blackwell, 2000

The Adventures of Five Hours

Text as revised and corrected by Samuel Tuke, put into modern spelling by Paul M S Hopkins with original scene descriptions, plus suggested alternatives (in round brackets)

DRAMATIS PERSONAE

Don Henrique, in love with Camilla, but rejected, choleric, jealous, revengeful.

Don Carlos, near kinsman to Don Henrique, a well-natured moral gentleman.

Don Octavio, in love with Porcia, but feigning to be in love with Camilla, a valiant and accomplished cavalier.

Don Antonio, contracted to Porcia by proxy, before he saw her, a soldier, haughty and of exact humour.

Porcia, sister to Don Henrique, ingenious, constant and severely virtuous.

Camilla, sister to Don Carlos, susceptible of love, but cautious of her honour.

Diego, servant to Octavio, bred a scholar, a great coward and a pleasant droll.

Flora, waiting-woman to Porcia, witty, contriving, and faithful to her mistress.

Ernesto and Sancho, servants to Don Antonio.

Sylvio, Geraldo, Pedro, Bernardino, Jago, servants to Don Henrique.

The Corregidor and attendants.

The scene: Seville

ACT ONE

(A room in) Don Henrique's house

[Enter Don Henrique]

Hen. How happy are the Men of easy Phlegm,
Born on the Confines of Indifference;
Holding from Nature the securest Tenure,
The Peaceful Empire o'er themselves; which we
The unhappy Men of Fire, without the aids
Of Mighty Reason, or Almighty Grace,
Are all our lives contending for in vain:
Tis evident, that Solid Happiness
Is founded on the Conquest of our Passions;
But since they are the Favourites of Sense,
Self-love bribes Reason still, in their defence:
Thus in a Calm I reason; but when crossed,
The Pilot quits the Helm, and I am tossed.

[Enter Silvio]

Sil. Sir, Don Carlos is without.
Hen. Wait on him in.

[Enter Carlos]

Car. Cousin, Methinks, this day hath longer seemed
Than usual; since 'tis so far advanced,
Without our seeing one another.
    Hen. If I had not been hindered by some business,
I should ere this have seen you, to have told you
Some pleasing News, I lately have received;
You have so often borne with my Distempers,
Tis fit that once, at least, you should partake,
Of my good humour.

Car. What cause soever has produced this change,
I heartily rejoice in the effect;
And may it long continue.

    Hen. I can inform you, by Experience now,
How great a satisfaction 'tis to find
A Heart and Head eased of a weighty care;
And for a Gentleman of my warm temper,
Jealous of the Honour of his Family
(As yet ne'er blemished) to be fairly freed
From the tuition of an Orphan Sister,
Rich, Beautiful, and Young.

    Car. You know, Don Henrique, for these thirteen years,
That I have been with the like Province charged,
An only Sister, by our Parents' Will,
(When they were called from their cares below)
Committed to my trust; much more exposed
To the great World than yours; and (Sir) unless
Nearness of blood deceive me, short of few
In those perfections which invite the Gallants:
Yet thanks to my Temper, Cousin, as well
As to her Virtue, I have seen her grow
Even from her Childhood, to her Dangerous Age,
Without the least disturbance to my Rest.
And when with equal Justice I reflect
On the great Modesty and Circumspection
Of Lovely Porcia, I conclude, that you
Might well have slept as undisturbed as I.

    Hen. Sir, I complain not of my Sister's Conduct;
But you know well, young Maids are so exposed
To the Invasion of audacious men,
And to the Malice of their envious Sex;
You must confess the Confines of their Fame
Are never safe, till guarded by a Husband.;
Tis true, discreet Relations ought to use
Preventions of all kinds, but Dear Carlos,
The Blemish once received, no Wash is good
For Stains of Honour, but the Offender's Blood.

    Car. You are too severe a Judge of point of Honour.

    Hen. And therefore having not long since received
The News that Don Antonio de Mendoza

Is likely to be here this Night from Flanders;
To whom my Sister, by the intervention
Of the Marquis D'Olivera, is contracted;
I will not close these eyes, till I have seen
Her, and my Cares, safe lodged within his Arms.
    Car. I find your Travels, Cousin, have not cured you
Of that innate Severity to Women;
Urged justly as a National Reproach
To all of us abroad; the rest o'th' world
Lament that tender Sex amongst us here,
Born only to be honourable Prisoners;
The greater Quality, the closer kept;
Which Cruelty is revenged upon our selves,
Whil'st by immuring those whom most we love,
We sing and sigh only to Iron Grates.
As cruel is that over-cautious Custom,
By Proxy, to contract Parties unknown
To one another; this is only fit
For Sovereign Princes, whose high Qualities
Will not allow of previous Interviews;
They sacrifice their Love to Public Good,
Consulting Interest of State, not Blood,
A Custom, which as yet, I never knew
Used amongst persons of a lower rank,
Without a sequel of sad Accidents.
Sir, Understand me right; I speak not this
By way of Prophecy; I am no Stranger
To Don Antonio's reputation,
Which I believe so just, I no way doubt
Your Sister's being happy in him.
    Hen. Don Carlos, let us quit this Argument;
I am now going to our Noble Friend
And Kinsman the Corregidor to see
If he'll oblige us with his company
At my Sister's Wedding; will you come along?
    Car. Most willingly; as soon as I have brought
My Sister hither, who has given this Evening
To her Cousin Porcia.
    Hen. I have some business, Cousin, by the way,
I'll go before, and wait you i'th' Piazza.

Your servant, Sir.
[Henrique waits on him to the door]
[Exit Carlos.

Hen. This Kinsman is my bosom friend, and yet
Of all Men living, I must hide from him
My deep resentments of his Sister's scorn;
That cruel Maid, to wound me to the Heart,
Then close her Ears against my just complaints;
But though as yet I cannot heal my wound,
I may by my Revenge upon my Rival
Divert the pain; and I will drive it home;
There's in Revenge a Balm, which will appease
The present grief, and Time cure the disease.
[Exit Henrique.

[Enter Porcia]

Por. My heart is so oppressed, with fear and grief,
That it must break, unless it finds relief
The man I love, is forced to fly my sight,
And like a Parthian, kills me in his flight,
One whom I never saw, I must embrace,
Or else destroy the honour of my Race.
A Brother's Care, more cruel than his Hate;
O how perplexed are the Intrigues of Fate!

[Enter Carlos and Camilla]

Car. Cousin, I thought my Sister's company
Would not displease you, whil'st I wait upon
Your Brother in a Visit.
Por. Sir, You oblige me with a welcome favour;
I rather should have styled it Charity,   [Aside.
To bring a friend to her, whose cruel Fate
Has robbed her of herself.
Cam. Methinks, 'tis pity that a Wall should make
The Houses two, of Friends so entirely one,
As you, and I, and our two Brothers are.
Por. If it be true, that Lovers live much more
There where they Love, than where they Breath, I'm sure
No Walls can sever us, we are still together.
Car. Were I not much engaged, I would not quit

So sweet a Conversation; but, Sister,
At my Return I'll wait upon you home.
   Por. For this night, Cousin, pray let her be mine,
I beg it of you both.
   Car. You may command, we are both yours.

                         [Exit Carlos.

   Por. My dear Camilla, how I longed to have thee,
        [Porcia throws herself on Camilla's neck]
Where freely breathing out my Grief, I might
Some Mitigation from thy Pity find;
But since there's no true Pity without Pain;
Why should I ease, by thy Affliction gain?
   Cam. Ah Porcia! if Compassion suffering be,
And to condole be Pain; my Destiny
Will full Revenge in the same kind afford,
Should I, but my unequalled griefs relate,
And you, but equally participate.
   Por. If yours, as mine, from Love-disasters rise,
Our Fates are more allied than Families.
   Cam. What, to our Sex, and blooming Age can prove
An Anguish worthy of our Sighs, but Love?
   Por. Tis true, Camilla, were your Fate like mine,
Hopeless to Hold, unable to Resign.
   Cam. Let's tell our Stories, then we soon shall see,
Which of us two excels in misery.
   Por. Cousin, Agreed.
   Cam. Do you begin then.
   Por. You know, Camilla, best, how generously,
How long, and how discreetly, Don Octavio
Has served me; and what trials of his Faith,
And Fervour I did make, ere I allowed him
The least Hope to sustain his noble Love.
Cousin, All this you know; 'twas in your House
We had our Interviews; where you were pleased
To suffer feigned Addresses to your self,
To cover from my watchful Brother's eyes
The passion which Octavio had for me.
   Cam. My memory in this needs no refreshing.
   Por. And how one Evening (Oh that fatal hour)

My Brother passing by Don Carlos' House,
With his great Friend, and Confidant Don Pedro,
Did chance to see the unfortunate Octavio,
In your Balcony, entertaining me;
Whom, not believing there, he took for you;
My Back being towards him, and both Dressed alike;
Enraged with Jealousy, this cruel Man
(To whom all Moderation is unknown)
Resolves to stamp all your neglects of him,
In his supposed Rival, poor Octavio's heart;
They take their Stand i'the corner of our Street;
And after some short time, Octavio,
Free from Suspicion, as Design of ill,
Retires; they assault him, and in his own Defence
He kills Don Pedro, and is forced to fly;
My Brother cruelly pursues him still,
With such insatiate thirst after Revenge,
That nothing but Octavio's blood can quench;
Covering this his ill Nature and Suspicion
With the Resentment of Don Pedro's death.
    Cam. Is this the sum of your sad Story, Porcia?
Is this all?
    Por. No, no, Camilla, 'tis the Prologue only,
The Tragedy will follow. This Brother
To whose impetuous Will, my deceased Parents
(May their Souls rest in peace) having condemned
Me, and my Fortune; treats me like a Slave;
So far from suffering me to make my choice,
That he denounces Death if I refuse;
And now to frustrate all my hopes at once,
Has very lately made me sign a Contract
To one in Flanders, whom I never saw;
And is this night (they say) expected here.
    Cam. Is such a Rigour possible, dear Porcia?
    Por. Was ever misery like mine, Camilla?
Reduced to such Extremes, past all Relief
If I acquaint my Brother with my Love
To Octavio, the man whom he most hates,
I must expect the worst effects of Fury;
If I endeavour to forget Octavio,

Even that Attempt renews his Memory,
And heightens my Disquiet; If I Refuse
To Marry, I am lost; If I Obey,
I cast Octavio, and my Self away.
Two such Extremes of Ill, no Choice admit;
Each seems the worst; on which Rock shall I split?
Since if I Marry, I cannot survive;
And not to Marry; were to Die alive.
    Cam. Your Story I confess is strangely moving;
Yet if you could my Fortune weigh with yours,
In Scales of equal sensibility;
You would not change your Sufferings for mine.
    Por. What can there be in Nature more afflicting?
Than to be torn from the Object of my Love?
And forced to embrace a man, whom I must hate.
    Cam. Have you not known that Object of your Love?
And entertained the Person you esteem?
Have you not heard, and answered to his Sighs?
Has he not borne his part in all your Cares?
Do not you live, and reign within his heart?
    Por. I doubt no more his Faith, than my hard Fate.
    Cam. Tell me, dearest Porcia, if I love one,
Whom I shall never see, suffering as much
Without the means of e'er expressing it,
As what I suffer is above Expression;
If all my Sighs wander in fleeting Air,
And ne'er can reach his Ears, for whom they're formed;
If all my Passion, all my killing Cares,
Must be for ever to their Cause unknown;
If their sad weight must sink me to my Grave,
Without one Groan, that he can ever hear,
Or the least Hope, that I should e'er obtain
Ease by his Pity, or Cure by his Disdain;
If this the State of my misfortune be,
As Heaven that has decreed it, knows it is,
Say, dearest Porcia, do you envy me?
    Por. What over-cruel Laws of decency
Have struck you dumb? Have you misplaced your Love,
On such a Party as you dare not own?
    Cam. No, no; the Cause is worthy of the Effect;

For though I had no Passion for this Person,
I were Ungrateful, if I should not give
The first place in my heart to such high Merit.
    Por. If he has been so happy to deserve Your Love,
Why are not you so Just, to let
Him know it?
    Cam. Tis impossible; Ah! that dismal word
Clearly states the difference of our Fortunes:
You, in your first Adventure, have been crossed.
But I, before I can set out, am lost.
    Por. Pray make me comprehend this Mystery.
    Cam. Tis to open my wounds afresh, dear Porcia,
But you must be obeyed –
                  [After a little pause]
His Excellence the Conde d'Oniate
Being sent Ambassador to the Emperor,
We having th' honour to be near allied
To his Lady, who went with Him; my Brother
Was desired, by her, to make that Journey:
Whose tenderness for me, not suffering him
To let me stay behind, I was engaged;
And treated by the Ambassadress, my Cousin,
With more respect, than I could ever merit.
    Por. She's a Lady, famed for great Civility.
    Cam. We had not passed much time in the Emperor's
    Court,
When my dear Brother, unexpectedly,
By urgent Business, was called back to Seville;
In our return (passing too near a Garrison
Of the Enemies) our Convoy was surprised
And routed by a Party of their Horse.
    Por. Camilla, You begin to raise my fears.
    Cam. We being Prisoners, were hurried straight away
To the Enemy's Quarters, where my ill Fate
Made me appear too pleasing to the Eyes
Of their Commander; who, at first approach,
Pretends to parley in a Lover's Style,
Protesting that my Face had changed our Fortunes,
And him my Captive made: But finding soon
How little he advanced in his Design,

By Flattery, and by his feigned submission;
He shifts his Person, calls me his Prisoner,
And swears my Virgin Treasure was his Prize;
But yet protests he had much rather owe it
To my Indulgence than his own Good Fortune;
And so through Storms and Calms, the Villain still
Pursues his Course to his accursed End;
But finding me inflexible, to his Threats
As well as Fawnings, he resolves to use
The last, and uncontrolled Argument
Of Impious Men in power, Force.
   Por. Ah poor Camilla, where was your Brother
At a time of such distress?
   Cam. My Brother? He, alas, was long before
Borne away from me, in the first Encounter;
Where having gallantly behaved himself,
As well became his Nation, and his Name,
Remained sore wounded in another House.
   Por. Prithee make haste to free me from this fright.
   Cam. The Brute approaches, and by Violence
Endeavours to accomplish his Intent;
I invoke my Guardian Angel, and resist,
But with unequal force, though Rage supplied
Those Spirits which my Fear had put to flight;
At length grown faint with crying out and striving,
I spied a Dagger by the Villain's side,
Which snatching boldly out, as my last refuge,
With his own Arms wounded the Savage Beast,
He, at the stroke, unseized me, and gave back;
So Guilt produces Cowardice, then I,
The Dagger pointing to my Breast, cried out,
Villain, keep off, for if thou do'st persist,
I'll be myself both Sacrifice and Priest.
I boldly now defy thy Lust and Hate;
She that dares Choose to die, may Brave her Fate.
   Por. O how I Love and Envy thee at once,
          [Porcia starts to her and kisses her]
Go on brave Maid.
   Cam. Immediately the Drums and Trumpets sound,
Pistols go off, and a great Cry to Arms,

To Arms: The Lustful Satyr flies; I stand
Fixed with amazement to the Marble Floor,
Holding my Guardian Dagger up aloft,
As if the Ravisher had threatened still.

 Por. I fancy thee, Camilla, in that brave posture,
Like a Noble Statue, which I remember
Once to have seen, of the enraged Juno,
When she had robbed Jove of his Thunderbolt.

 Cam. Freed from this Fright, my Spirits flowed so fast,
To the forsaken Channels of my Heart,
That they, who by their orderly Access
Would have supported life, by Throngs oppress.
O'ercharg'd with Joy, I fell into a swoon;
And that which happened during this Interval,
Is not within the Circle of my Knowledge.

 Por. You've raised me to a mighty expectation;
Will the Adventure answer it, Camilla?

 Cam. At my return to life, opening my eyes,
Think, dearest Porcia, how I was astonished
To find there kneeling by my side, a Man
Of a most Noble Form, who bowing to me,
Madam (says he) you're welcome to the World;
Pardon, I pray, the Boldness of a Stranger,
Who humbly sues to you to continue in it;
Or if you needs will leave us, stay at least
Until I have Revenged your wrongs, and then
I'll wait upon you to the other world;
For you withdrawn, this will a Desert seem,
And Life a Torment.

 Por. High Gallantry, Cousin, for the first Address.

 Cam. 'Twas so surprising, that my Confusion
Checked my Reply; but I suppose my Looks
Did speak the grateful Language of my heart;
For I perceived an Air of Joy enlighten
His Manly Face; but, Oh! how soon 'twas clouded,
By fresh Alarms; We heard the Soldiers cry,
"Where's Antonio? The Enemy is rallied,
And coming on to give a second Charge";
He started up, and with a Mien that marked
The Conflict 'twixt his Honour and his Love;

Madam, (says he) the Soul was never yet
With such Convulsion from the Body torn,
As I from you; but it must ne'er be said,
That Don Antonio de Mendoza
Follows those in Dangers, whom he ought to lead;
Thus, the Vanquished Conqueror disappeared,
Leaving that Image stamped upon my Heart,
To which I all the Joys must sacrifice
Of the poor Remnant of my wretched Life;
If properly to live I may be said,
                    [She puts her handkerchief to her eyes]
When all my hopes of seeing him are dead.
   Por. Though you have kept this part of your Adventure
Still from me -
   Cam. And from every Body living -
   Por. I have observed the Signs of Smothered Grief
I've often seen those Lovely Eyes much swollen,
Those are true tears, Camilla, which are stolen.
But what said you was his Name, Camilla?
   Cam. Antonio de Mendoza.
   Por. Oh Heavens! Antonio de Mendoza.

                    [Enter Henrique]

   Hen. I'm pleased to find you speaking of your Husband.
   Cam. What's that I hear? Her Husband?   [Aside.
   Hen. Have you the Letter ready, I desired you
To write to him? I'll send a Servant with it,
To meet him on the way, 'twill shew Respect.
   Por. You know my obedience, Brother.
   Hen. Tis well, Sister.

                    [Enter Sylvio]

   Syl. Sir, Here's a Servant of Don Antonio
Newly alighted at the Gate; he's come
Post from his Master, charged with Letters for you.
   Hen. I could not have received more welcome News,
Go, bring him in; Sister you may withdraw.

                              [Exit Porcia and Camilla.

[Sylvio ushers in Ernesto]

Ern. Sir, Don Antonio kisses your hands,
And send me to present this Letter to you.

[He gives a letter to Don Henrique]

[Don Henrique opens it,
and having read it to himself, says]

Hen. I'm glad to find by his Letter he's in health.
Yet methinks, Friend, he writes but doubtfully,
Of being here this night, as I expected.
 Ern. His Letter, I suppose Sir, speaks his purpose.
 Hen. I'll answer it, and dispatch you presently.
In the meantime go make him welcome, Sylvio.

[Exit Sylvio and Ernesto.

I would to Heaven he were arrived; I grow
Each minute more impatient: As Bodies
Near their Centre move with more violence,
So, when we approach the Ends of our Designs,
Our Expectations are the more Intense
And our fears greater of all cross Events.

[Exit Henrique.

[Enter Sylvio, Ernesto, Geraldo, Pedro, Bernardino,
Jago, with some cups of chocolate]

Syl. Methinks Comrade, a sup of Chocolate
Is not amiss, after a tedious Journey,
Your Master's Health, Sir.

[He drinks]

 Ern. I'll do you reason, Sir.
 Syl. Pray how long is't, Brother, since you left Spain?
 Ern. Tis now five years and upwards, since I went
From Seville, with my Master, into Flanders,
The King's Fencing School; where all his Subjects
Given to Fighting, are taught the use of Arms,
And notably kept in breath.

Syl. Your Master, I am sure, has got the Fame
To be a Perilous Man in that rough Trade.
  Ern. He's a brave Soldier, Envy must confess it.
  Ped. It seems so, faith, since merely by the force
Of his great Reputation, he can take
Our bright young Mistress in without a Siege.
  Ern. If I mistake not, she will be revenged
On him, ere long, and take him too, by the force
Of her rare Wit and Beauty.
  Ped. She has a fair portion, Sir, of both,
I dare Assure you.
  Syl. But prithee, Brother, instruct us a little,
Tell us, what kind of Country is this Holland,
That's so much talked of, and so much Fought for?
  Ern. Why, friend, 'tis a huge Ship at Anchor, fraught
With a sort of Creatures, made up of Turf,
And Butter.
  Ped. Pray, Sir, what do they drink in that Country.
Tis said, there's neither Fountains there, Nor Vines.
  Ern. This is the Butler, sure, by his apt question.   [Aside.
Friend, they drink there a certain muddy Liquor,
Made of that Grain, with which you feed your Mules.
  Ped. What? Barley? Pray can that Juice quench
Their thirst?
  Ern. You'd scarce believe it could, did you but see
How oft they drink.
  Ped. But methinks, that should make them drunk, Comrade.
  Ern. Indeed most Strangers are of that opinion,
But they Themselves believe it not, because
They're so often drunk.
  Ger. A Nation sure of Walking Tuns; the World
Has not the like.
  Ern. Pardon me, Friend, there is but a great Ditch
Betwixt them, and just such another Nation.
If these Good fellows would but Join, and drink
That dry, i'faith they might shake hands.
  Ger. Prithee, friend, can these Dutch Borracio's Fight?
  Ern. They can do even as well, for they can Pay
Those that can fight.
  Syl. But where, I pray Sir, do they get their Money?

Ern. Oh Sir, they have a thriving Mystery;
They Cheat their Neighbouring Princes of their Trade,
And then they buy their Subjects for their Soldiers.
    Syl. Methinks our Armies should beat these Butter-boxes
Out of the world.
    Ern. Trust me Brother, they'll sooner beat our Armies,
Out of their Country; Why, ready Money, Friend,
Will do much more, in Camps, as well as Courts,
Than a ready wit, I dare assure you.
    Ger. Methinks, Comrade, our King should have more Money,
Than these Dutch Swabbers. He's Master o'the Indies,
Where Money grows.
    Ern. But they have Herrings, Friend, which I assure you,
Are worth our Master's Mines.
    Ger. Herrings! Why what a Devil, do they grow
In their Country?
    Ern. No faith, they fish 'em on the English Coast,
And fetch their Salt from France, then they pickle 'em,
And sell'em all o'er the world.
    Ger. 'S'life, these Rascals live by Cookery.
    Ern. This is the coddled Cook, I've found him out.   [Aside.
    Ber. What kind of Beds Sir have they in that Country?
    Ern. This, I dare swear's, the Groom o'the Chamber.   [Aside.
Sir, they have certain Niches in their walls,
Where they climb up a Nights, and there they stew,
In their own Grease, till Morning.
    Jag. Pray Sir, Give me leave to ask you one question,
What manner of Women have they in that Country?
    Ern. The Gentleman-Usher upon my life.   [Aside.
Pray excuse me, Sir, we Gentlemen Soldiers
Value ourselves upon our Civility
To that soft Sex; and in good faith, they are
The softest of that Sex, I ever met with.
    Jag. Does any of our Spaniards ever marry with 'em?
    Ern. Yes, some Lean Families, that have a mind
To lard their Progeny.
    Syl. What, a God's name, could come into the Heads
Of this People, to make them Rebel?
    Ern. Why Religion; that came into their Heads
A God's name.

Ger. But what a Devil made the Noblemen
Rebel? They never mind Religion.
   Ern. Why that which made the Devil himself Rebel,
Ambition.
   Syl. This is a pleasant Fellow;   [Aside.
I find you Gentlemen Soldiers want not wit.
   Ern. Not when we're well paid Sir, but that's so seldom,
I find that Gentleman wants wit that is
A Soldier: your Company's very good,
But I have business which requires Dispatch.
   Ped Will you not mend your Draught before you go?
   Ern. I thank you, Sir, I have done very well.
   All. Your servant, your servant.

                              [Exeunt.

         [Enter Camilla, Porcia, Flora]

   Por. Was e'er Disaster like to mine Camilla?
   Cam. Was e'er Misfortune Porcia, like to mine?
   Por. That I must never see Octavio more.
   Cam. That I again must Don Antonio see,
Yet never see him mine.
   Por. I, to be married to the Man I hate.
   Cam. And I, to have the Man I love, torn from me.
   Por. I am by Robbing of my Friend, undone.
   Cam. I, for not hindering of the Theft, am lost.
   Por. Ye Powers, who these entangled fortunes give,
Instruct us how to Die, or how to Live.

              [She weeps]

   Cam. Cousin, when we should Act, then to Complain
Is Childishly to beat the Air in vain.
These descants on our Griefs only perplex;
Let's seek the Remedy; you know, our Sex
This Honour bears from Men, in Exigents
Of Love, never to want Expedients.
   Por. You have awakened me, give me your Veil.

   [Porcia takes off Camilla's veil, and puts it on herself]

Quickly, dear Cousin quickly, and you, Flora,
Run presently, and see whether my Brother
Be settled to dispatch Antonio's Man.

[Exit Flora.

    Cam. What mean you Porcia?
    Por. If once my Brother be set down to write,
I may securely reckon one Hour mine;
For he is so extravagantly Jealous,
That he Distrusts the sense of his own words;
And will weigh a Subscription to a scruple,
Lest he should wrong his Family by his Style;
Therefore I'll serve myself of this Occasion
To see Octavio, and to let him know;
That all our hopes are ready to expire,
Unless he finds some prompt Expedient
For our Relief.
    Cam. Pray how, and where do you hope to speak
with him?
    Por. At his own House, where he lies yet concealed,
Tis not far off and I will venture thither.
    Cam. Do you know the way?
    Por. Not very well, but Flora's a good Guide.

[Enter Flora hastily]

Flo. Oh Madam! He's coming already.
Por. Ah spiteful Destiny! Come, let's retire
Into my Chamber, Cousin.

[Exit Porcia and Camilla.

[Enter Henrique and Ernesto]

    Hen. If you desire to see her, Friend, you may.
    Ern. I should be glad to acquaint my Master, Sir,
That I have had the honour to see his Bride.
    Hen. Where's your Lady, Flora?
    Flo. She's in her Chamber, Sir.
    Hen. Tell her, Antonio's Man attends her here.
To do his Duty to her, ere he goes.

[Exit Flora.

[To Ernesto]
Stay here; you'll find her with a Kinswoman
In her home-dress, without a Veil, but you
Are privileged, by your Relation, for this access,
I'll go dispatch my Letter.

[Exit Henrique.

[Enter Camilla, Porcia, and Flora]
[Ernesto addresses himself to Camilla, seeing her
without a veil]

Ern. Madam, I have been bold to beg the Honour
Of seeing your Ladyship, to make myself
More welcome to my Lord, at my return.
Por. A rare mistake, further it, dear Camilla.   [Aside.
Who knows what Good this Error may produce?
Cam. Friend, in what state left you your Lord and mine?
Ern. As happy, as the Hopes of being yours
Could make him, Madam.
Cam. I would the Master were as easily deceived   [Aside.
I pray present my humble service to him;
And let him know, that I am very glad
He has passed his Journey so successfully,
Give him the Letter Flora, farewell Friend.

[Exit Camilla, Porcia, and Flora.

Ern. Now by my life, she is a lovely Lady;
My Master will be ravished with her Form,
I hope this blind Bargain, made by Proxy,
May prove as happy a Marriage, as those
Made after the Old Fashion, chiefly for Love;
And that this unseen Beauty may have Charms,
To bring him back to his right wits again,
From his wild Ravings on an unknown Dame,
Whom, as he fancies (once upon a time)
He recovered from a Trance, that's to say
From a sound Sleep, which makes him Dream e'er since.
I'll hasten to him with this pleasing News.

[Exit Ernesto.

[Enter Camilla, Porcia, Flora]

Cam. My Melancholy could hardly hinder me
From laughing at the formal Fool's mistake;
But tell me, Did not I present your Person
With rare assurance? The way for both to thrive,
Is to make me your Representative.
   Por. Most willingly, and I am confident,
When you, your Charms shall to his heart apply,
You all your Rivals safely may defy.
   Cam. I wish I could be vain enough to hope it.
But, Cousin, my Despairs are so extreme,
I can't be flattered, though but in a Dream.
   Flo. Madam, do we go, or what do you resolve on?
   Por. I must resolve, but know not what to choose.
   Cam. Cousin, take heed, I am afraid you venture
Too much, your Brother cannot tarry long;
And, if at his return he finds you missing -
   Por. You've reason - the opportunity is lost.
What is't a'clock, Flora?
   Flo. I think near Seven, for the Clock struck Six
Just as Camilla entered the Chamber.
   Por. Quick then, Flora, fetch your Veil, you shall carry
My Tablets to Octavio; there he'll find
The Hour and Place where I would have him meet.

[Exit Flora.

   Cam. Tis well resolved; but where do you design
Your Meeting?
   Por. In the Remotest part of all the Garden,
Which answers (as you know) to my Apartment;
And Flora has the Key of the back door.
   Cam. As the Case stands, you choose the fittest place.

[Flora returns veiled]

   Por. Cousin, I beg your patience whil'st I write.

[Porcia writes in her tablets]

   Cam. You, Mistress Flora, by this Accident
May chance to see your faithful lover, Diego.

Flo. He is a faithful Lover of himself,
Without a Rival, Madam.
    Cam. Damsel, Your words and thoughts hardly agree;
For could we see his Image in your Heart,
'Twould be a fairer far, than e'er his Glass Reflected.
    Flo. Madam, I am not yet so very old,
That I should dote.
    Cam. Nor yet so very young, but you may love.
Dotage and Love are Cousin-germans, Flora.
    Flo. Yes, when we love, and are not loved again;
                 [Smiling]
For else, I think they're not so near a kin.

Cam. I have touched a Nettle, and stung myself	[Aside.

Por. Make all the haste you can, pray Flora.

Flo. Madam, I'll fly.	
Should I not play my part, I were to blame.	[Aside.

Since all my Fortune's betted on her Game.
Madam, has Octavio the other Key
Belonging to the Tablets?
    Por. Yes, yes, I pray make haste.

                                   [Exit Flora.

    Cam. Cousin, Pray call for Mirabel, and let her
Divert us with a Song.
    Por. Who waits there?

                   [Enter Page]

Page, Bid Mirabel come in and Floridor
With his Lute, and send in somebody with Chairs.

                                 [Exit Page.

    Cam. Pray Cousin, let her sing her newest Air.
    Por. What you please.
    Cam. Tell me, prithee, whose Composition was it?
    Por. Guess, and I'll tell you true.

               [They bring in chairs]

    Cam. Octavio's.
    Por. You are i'the right.

           [Enter Mirabel and Floridor]

Mirabel, sing Mistaken Kindness.

The Song

Can Luciamira so mistake,
To persuade me to fly;
Tis cruel-kind for my own sake,
To counsel me to die.
Like those faint souls, who cheat themselves of breath,
And die for fear of death.

Since Love's the Principle of Life,
And you, the Object loved,
Let's, Luciamira, end this strife,
I cease to be removed.
We know not what they do, are gone from hence,
But here we love by sense.

If the Platonicks who would prove
Souls without Bodies love,
Had, with respect, well understood
The Passion's i'the Blood,
They had suffered Bodies to have had their part,
And seated Love i'the Heart.

Por. What discord there's in Music, when the Heart,
Untuned by trouble, cannot bear a part.
    Cam. In vain we seek Content in outward things,
Tis only from within where Quiet springs.

                                                   [Exeunt.

            (Alternative ending from first edition)

    Por. Yes, yes, I pray, make haste.

                                               [Exit Flora.

Let us retire, Camilla. A little rest
And Meditation, may new aids suggest.

                                               [Exeunt.

ACT TWO

A street in Seville

[Enter Don Antonio and Sancho in riding clothes]

San. Sir, we are arrived in very good time.
Ant. I did not think it would have been so soon
By an hour at least, but Lovers ride apace.
Why smile you Sancho?
San. Faith at the Novelty of your Amours,
To fall in love with one you hardly saw,
And marry one you never saw, 'tis pretty,
But we poor Mortals have another Method.
Ant. You're very pleasant, Friend, but is not this
The Market Place behind the Jacobins?
San. Yes Sir.
Ant. Tis here I charged Ernesto to expect me.
San. Since you are here, Sir, earlier than you thought,
Why might you not go shift you at the Post-house,
And be returned before Ernesto comes?
Howe'er, 'tis better, that he wait for you,
Than you for him, i'the open Street.
Ant. Tis well thought on; Come let's go then.

[Exeunt.

[Enter Don Octavio and Diego]

Oct. Come, Diego, 'tis now time to quit our Dens,
And to begin our Chase.
Die. Of what, Sir? Bats, or Owls, now the Sun's set:
Call you this making of Love? why methinks,
Tis more like making of War; marching all night
In Arms, as if we designed to Beat up
The Enemy's Quarters.

Oct. Why, would not you venture as much for Flora?

Die. No in good faith Sir; I shall venture enough,
If e'er I marry her; I'll run no hazard,
(By my good will) before-hand.

    Oct. That's from your fear, not prudence, Diego.

    Die. Sir, you may call it what you please, but I
Dare boldly say, there lives not in the world
A more Valiant Man, than I, whil'st Danger
Keeps its due Distance; but when saucily
It presses on, then (I confess) 'tis true,
I have a certain tenderness for life,
Which checks my ardour, and inclines my prudence
Timely to withdraw.

    Oct. Your Style is wondrous civil to yourself;
How you soften that harsh word, called Cowardice;
But the danger is not always evident,
When you are pleased, my Friend, to run away.

    Die. It may be so, Sir, not to Vulgar eyes;
But I have such a piercing sight, that I
Discover Perils out of others' Ken;
Which, they not seeing soon enough to shun,
Are forced to encounter; and then their struggling
Is, by the unwary world, taken for Courage.

    Oct. Who's truly valiant, will be always so.

    Die. Who's wisely valiant will avoid the Foe.

    Oct. You have more Light, Diego, I see than Heat;
But I'll allow your Wit and Honesty
To come to Composition for your want
Of Courage.

    Die. I have Courage enough for the Profession
To which my Parents did design me.

    Oct. Why what was that?

    Die. An Advocate; I could have acted Choler
In my Clients' sight, and when his back was turned,
Have hugged the Lawyer of the adverse Party;
And if I mistake not, they sell their Breath:
Much dearer than you Soldiers do your Blood.
Tis true you get Honour, a fine light food,
For delicate Complexions; but I have
Known some Captains of plain Stomachs starve upon it.

Oct. The Varlet's i'the right. [Aside.
How came it about
You were not of this thriving Trade?
    Die. After I had spent seven years at Salamanca,
My Father, a rich Merchant of this City,
Was utterly undone, by that Damned Englishman,
With whom we fright our Children.
    Oct. Who Captain Drako? Was he a Pirate?
    Die. He had been so on this side of the Line.
    Oct. Tis strange that War and Peace should have
    degrees
Of Latitude; one would have thought they should
Have been the same all o'er the world; but what's this
To my Amours? I trifle away my time.
Was ever Lover's Fate so rude as mine?
Condemned to Darkness, forced to hide my Head,
As well as Love? and to spite me the more,
Fortune has Contradictions reconciled,
I am at once a Prisoner, and exiled.

[Enter Antonio and Sancho]

    Ant. Methinks, Ernesto should not tarry long,
If not already come; Sancho, how call you
The Street there just before us? Where you see
Yon Gentleman with his Cloak o'er his face?
I have lost all my measures of this Town.
    San. I am as much to seek as you, Sir.
    Ant. Let us go to him, Sancho, and enquire;
He has a notable good Mien; I ne'er
Saw an Air more like Octavio's.
    Oct. Unless my eyes do very much deceive me,
That's Don Antonio; if it be he, Diego,
There is no danger in his knowing us:
He was my Comrade when I first bore Arms,
        [Octavio lets fall his cloak from before his face]
Tis He.
    Ant. You injure me Octavio, to be so long
A knowing one, who's so entirely yours.

[They embrace]

Oct. Your presence in this place, Noble Antonio,
Was so unexpected, I hardly durst
Believe my eyes; When came you to this Town?

Ant. I am just now arrived.

Oct. I joy to see you here, but should have thought
It likelier to have heard of you at Court,
Pursuing there the Recompences due
To your great Merit.

Ant. That is no place for men of my Morality;
I have been taught, Octavio, to deserve,
But not to seek Reward; that does profane
The Dignity of Virtue; if Princes,
For their own Interests, will not advance
Deserving Subjects, they must raise Themselves,
By a brave Contempt of Fortune.

Oct. Rigorous Virtue! which makes us to deserve,
Yet suffer the neglect of those we serve.

Ant. Virtue to Interest, has no regard;
Nor is it Virtue, if we expect reward.

Oct. If for their service, Kings our Virtues press,
Is no pay due to Valour and Success?

Ant. When we gave up our Persons to their Will,
We gave, with those, our Valour, Fortune, Skill.

Oct. But this Condition tacitly was meant,
Kings should adjust Reward, and Punishment.

Ant. Kings are the only Judges of Desserts
And our Tribunal's seated in their Hearts.

Oct. But if they judge, and act amiss, what then?

Ant. They must account to the Powers above, not Men.

Oct. Then we must suffer.

Ant. Yes; if we reject
Their Power as too great; we must erect
A greater to Control them; and thus we
Instead of shrinking, swell the Tyranny.

Oct. We obey for fear then.

Ant. True, 'Tis only above
Where Power is Justice, and Obedience Love.

Oct. I'm glad to find, in you, the seeds yet left
Of steady Virtue; may they bring forth fruit
Fit to Illustrate, and Instruct the Age.

Let me once more embrace you; Welcome brave Man,
Both the Delight, and Honour of your Friends.

[Embraces Antonio]

Ant. You will give me leave, Sir, to distinguish
Betwixt your Judgment, and Civility.
Oct. He has not lived i'the reach of Public Fame,
Who is a stranger to your Character.
This is my House, be pleased, Sir, to go in,
And make it yours; though truly at present
I am but in an ill Condition
To receive the Honour of such a Guest;
Having by an unlucky Accident
Been forced of late to keep myself concealed.
Ant. I humbly thank you, Sir, but cannot yet
Receive your Favour, for I must stay here
Expecting the Return of one I sent
Before me to my Brother-in-Law's.
Oct. Have you a Brother-in-Law in Seville?
You surprise me much.
Ant. It is most true, Octavio, I come hither
A Married Man, as much as Friends can make me.
Oct. Since it imports you not to miss your Servant,
Let us stay here without, until he comes;
And then go in, and rest yourself awhile.
But, How go our Affairs in Flanders?
Ant. I left our Armies in a better State
Than formerly.
Oct. And your Governor, the Duke of Alva,
I suppose, in great Reputation?
Ant. The Honour of our Country, and the Terror
Of others; Fortune consulted Reason,
When she bestowed such Favours upon him.
Oct. And yet 'tis said, he loses ground at Court.
Ant. Tis possible; Under a Jealous Prince,
A great's as prejudicial, as an evil Fame.
Oct. They say he's cruel, even to Barbarity.
Ant. Tis Mercy, that, which they call Cruelty.
In a Civil War, in fertile Provinces,
(And the Sun sees not richer, than are these;)

The Soldier, especially the Auxiliary,
Whose trade it is to fight for Salary;
Is bribed by gain, the Rebels' lives to spare,
That mutual Quarter may prolong the War
Till this slow Fever has consumed their force,
And then, they'll fall to our Rival France, of course.
War made in earnest, maketh War to cease,
And vigorous Prosecution hastens Peace.
    Oct. You've made me comprehend his Conduct;
He's sure as great a Politician as a Soldier.
    Ant. Loyalty's his Centre, his Circumference Glory;
And to after Ages, he'll show great in Story.
    Oct. And our good friend the Marquis d'Olivera,
In High esteem?
    Ant. The boast of our Army; he has exceeded
Hope, and made flattery impossible.
    Oct. They say he did Wonders at the Siege of Mons.
    Ant. You mean (as I suppose) at the pursuit
O'the German Army led by the Prince of Orange:
Indeed his Courage, and his Conduct there
Were very signal.
    Oct. You'll much oblige me, if whilst you expect
Your Servant here, I might learn from yourself
Some few Particulars of your own Actions;
Fame speaks loudly of them, but not distinctly.
    Ant. Fame, like Water, bears up the lighter things,
And lets the weighty sink; I do not use
To speak in the first Person; but, if you needs
Will have a Story to fill up the time,
I'll tell you an Adventure of mine own,
Where you'll find Love so intermixed with Arms,
That (I am confident) 'twill raise your wonder,
How being prepossessed with such a Passion,
I should (upon Prudential motives only)
Be engaged (as now you find me) to Marry
A Lady whom I never saw.
    Oct. The Person, and the Subject, Sir, both challenge
My best attention.
    Ant. [After a little pause]
The following Evening to that glorious Day

Wherein the Duke of Alva gained such Fame,
Against the Cautelous Nassau; some Horse
Were sent from the Army, under my command
To cover the Limbourg Frontiers, much exposed
To the Enemy's Inroads; my Troops scarce lodged,
I received Intelligence, that a Party
Of the Enemy (about two hundred Horse)
Were newly come to a Village three Leagues off,
Intending there to lodge; Immediately
We sound to Horse, and March to their Surprise
So luckily, that by the break of day
Their Quarters were on fire.
    Oct. You had been taught, Sir, by your wife General,
That Diligence in Execution, is
(Even above Fortune) Mistress of Success.
    Ant. They made but faint Resistance; some were slain,
Some perished in the Fire, others Escaped,
Giving the Alarm, in Quarters more remote,
To their Companions, drowned in Sleep, and Wine;
Who, at the Outcry, and the noise of Trumpets
Methinks I fancy starting from their Beds,
As pale, and wan, as from their Dormitories
Those the last Trump shall rouse, differing in this,
That those awake to live, but these to die.
    Oct. O how unsafe it is to be secure!
    Ant. Finding no more Resistance, I made haste
To a lofty Structure, which, as I conceived,
Was the likeliest Quarter for their Officer,
Led thither by Desire to rescue both,
Him, from the Soldiers' rage; That, from the Fire.
    Oct. A care most worthy of a Gallant Leader.
    Ant. But think, Octavio, how I was surprised,
When, entering a Pavilion i'the Garden,
I found a Woman of a matchless Form,
Stretched all along upon the Marble Floor.
    Oct. I easily can divine how such a heart,
As harbours in the brave Antonio's breast,
May suffer at so sad a Spectacle.
    Ant. At the first sight I did believe her dead;
Yet, in that State, so Aweful she appeared,

That I approached her, with as much Respect,
As if the Soul had animated still
That Body, which, though dead, scarce mortal seemed.
But as the Sun from our Horizon gone,
His Beams do leave a Tincture on the Skies,
Which shows it was not long since he withdrew;
So, in her lovely Face, there still appeared
Some scattered streaks of those Vermilion Beams,
Which used to irradiate that bright Firmament.
Thus did I find that Distressed Miracle,
Able to wound a Heart, as if Alive,
Uncapable to Cure it, as if Dead.
   Oct. I no more doubt your Pity, than your Wonder.
   Ant. My Admiration did suspend my Aid,
Till Passion joined to Pity, made me bold;
I kneeled, and took her in my Arms, then bowed
Her Body gently forward; at which instant,
A sigh stole from her; O the ravishing sound!
Which being a Symptom of remaining life,
Made me forget, that 'twas a sign of Grief.
At length she faintly opens her bright Eyes;
So breaks the day; and so do all the Creatures
Rejoice, as I did, at the new-born Light:
But as the Indians who adore the Sun,
Are scorched by's Beams, ere half his Race be Run;
So I, who did adore her rising Eyes,
Found myself wounded by those Deities.
   Oct. I am big with Expectation, pray Deliver me.
   Ant. From her fair hand a bloody Poniard fell,
Which she held fast during her Trance, as if
She had only needed Arms, whilst she did Sleep,
And trusted to her Eyes, when she did Wake.
What I said to her, being a production
Of mere Extasy, I remember not,
She made me no Reply, yet I discerned
In a Serener Air of her pale Face,
Some Lines of Satisfaction, mixed with Fear.
   Oct. Such looks in silence have an Eloquence.
But pray go on.
   Ant. Raised from the Ground, and to her self Returned,

I stepped a fitting distance back; as well
To gaze upon that lovely Apparition,
As to express Respect; when at that instant
The Trumpets sound a Charge; my Soldiers cry,
'Where is our Leader? Where's Antonio?'
My Love a while disputed with my Honour,
But that being the Longer settled Power
O'ercame; I joined my Troops, left in Reserve,
As they were ready to receive a Charge
From divers Squadrons of fresh Horse, who being
Quartered in Neighbouring Villages, had taken
Hotly the Alarm, and came (though then too late)
In succour of their Friends. Honour and Love
Had so inflamed my Heart, that I advanced
Beyond the Rules of Conduct, and received
So many wounds that I with faintness fell.
    Oct. How can this story end?
    Ant. My Soldiers beat the Enemy, and brought me off
Where Surgeons quickly cured my outward wounds,
But the remembrance of that Heroine,
My Inward Hurts keep bleeding still afresh;
Till by the business of the War constrained
To attend my Charge i'the Army, my despair
Of ever seeing her again conspiring
With the strong persuasions of Olivera,
I was at length, even forced to an Engagement
Of Marriage, with a lady of this City,
Rich, Noble, and, as they say, Beautiful.
And so you have me here come to Consummate
Those Nuptial Rites, to which my Interest,
And the Importunity of trusty Friends
O'errule my Judgment, though against my Heart.
    Oct. A wonderful Adventure! but pray, Sir,
May I not take the liberty to ask you,
Who may this noble Lady be, to whom
The Fates have destined so much happiness?
    Ant. I have no Reserves for you, Octavio,
Tis the Sister of –
        [Enter Ernesto, and Octavio retires hastily and
        covers his face with his cloak. Nodding to Octavio]

It is my servant, Sir.
   Oct. Step to Antonio, Diego, and desire him
To send him off.
   Ant. I will immediately. Well, Ernesto

       [Diego goes to Antonio, and whispers]

What good news? speak freely.
   Ern. Sir, as you charged me, I told your Brother-in-Law,
I thought you hardly could be there this Night,
He kisses your hands, and bad me tell you,
That he expects your coming with Impatience;
This Letter's from Don Henrique, the other's from
Your beauteous Bride, the most accomplished Person
I ever saw. My being of your train
Gave me the Privilege of a Domestic
To see her in her Chamber-dress, without
A Veil, either to cover Faults, or hide Perfections.
   Ant. Tell me truly, Is she so very handsome?
   Ern. Handsomer far in my opinion, Sir
Than all those Brussels Beauties, which you call
The Finished Pieces; but I'll say no more;
Let your own Eyes inform you; here's a Key
Of the Apartment, that's made ready for you;
A Lower Quarter, very nobly furnished,
That opens on Saint Vincent's Street.
   Ant. Give it me; and go you to the Post-house,
And take care that my things be brought from thence,

                           [Exit Ernesto.

Octavio, Will you go along with me,
And be a witness of my first Address?
   Oct. Sir, You choose in me an ill Companion
Of Lover's Interviews, or Nuptial Joys.
One, whose Misfortunes to such sad Extremes
Are heightened, that the very mentioning
Of Happy hours, serves only to Embitter
The Memory of my lost Joys.
   Ant. So very deep a sense of your Misfortunes,
Holds no Proportion with Octavio's mind.

[Enter Flora in haste, with tablets]

Flo. Where's your Master, Diego?

Die. There's some Ill towards, when this Bird appears, [Aside.
Do you not see him? You've lived too long a Maid.

Flo. Sir, I have something to say to you in private,
That requires haste.

Oct. What new Accident brings you hither, Flora?

Flo. These Tablets will inform you, Sir,

[Flora retires]

Die. Will you not stay for an Answer, Damsel?

Flo. Tis a Command, not a Question, Diego.

Die. Short, and sweet, Flora.

Oct. Good Flora stay a minute; I much fear
It is some new misfortune.

Die. Nay, Sir, you may be sure 'tis some Disaster,
Else it would ne'er have come so easily,
And so unsought for.

Oct. Will you allow me for a moment, Sir,
To step into my House, and read a Letter.

[Bowing to Antonio]

Ant. I'll wait upon you in, and stay your leisure.

[Exit all but Diego.

Die. These little black Books do more Devils raise,
Than all the Figures of the Conjurers.
This is some Missive from the Heroine.
If it ends not in Fighting I'll be hanged,
It is the Method of their dear Romances,
And Persons of their Rank make love by Book.
Curse on the Inventor of that damned device
Of Painting words, and speaking to our Eyes!
Had I a hundred Daughters, by this Light,
Not one of 'em should ever Read or Write.

[Enter Flora, and seems to go away in haste]

Here she comes again. 'Twas a quick dispatch.
A Word, Flora, or a kind glance at least.
What? grown cruel? Diego, nobody with you?

Flo. This is no time for fooling, friend.

Die. Nay, if you be so serious, fare you well;
But now I think on't better, I'll do the Honours
Of our Street, and bring you to the end on't.

Flo. I shall be well helped up with such a Squire.
If some wandering Knight should chance to assault you,
To bear away your Damsel, What would you do?

Die. I'd use no other weapon but a Torch;
I'd put aside your Veil, show him your Face;
That, I suppose, would guard us both.

Flo. Why, Do you think 'twould fright him, Diego?

Die. Oh no, 'twould charm him, Flora.

Flo. Well, such as 'tis, I'll venture it without
Engaging your known Valour, Good night.

                                                [Exit Flora.

[Enter Octavio and Antonio]

Oct. What may this be? I swear I cannot guess;
The Warning's short, but she must be obeyed;
The Hour draws near; I must go seek a friend,
Her words seem to imply need of a second;
T'were barbarous to engage Antonio,
Newly arrived, and come on such an Errand.   [Aside.
Noble Antonio, my confusion's great.
To tell you thus abruptly, I must leave you;
The occasion's indispensable.

Ant. I must not quit you, Sir, I know too well
The Laws of Honour, to desert you now:
When I perceive my friend in such disorder,
And all the marks that he is called to danger,
To leave him then…

Oct. It is a Summons from a Lady, Sir,
Whom I have loved with Passion, and Success;
To meet her in her Garden presently:
All is propitious on her part, and mine;
But she's so Guarded by a Tyrant Brother,
So naturally Jealous, and so Incensed
By a late Accident which I shall tell you,
That to assure you there would be no danger
In this Adventure were, Sir, to abuse you;

But for that very reason I am bound
Not to consent you should embark yourself,
In a business so directly opposite
To the occasion, which has brought you hither.
   Ant. I like the Omen at my first arrival;
To have the honour to serve so brave a Friend.
   Oct. You from a life of Perils, hither come
To find a Nuptial Bed, not seek a Tomb.
   Ant. My friend engaged, it never must be said
Antonio left him so, to go to bed.
   Oct. You're Married, and expose what's not your own.
   Ant. Wedded to Honour, that must yield to none.
   Oct. Honour makes me refuse your aid; We must
As well to friends, as to ourselves be just.
   Ant. He ought not to pretend to Friendship's name,
Who reckons not Himself and Friend the same.
   Oct. Friendship with Justice must not disagree,
That were to break the Virtues' harmony.
   Ant. Friendship is Justice, for, whene'er we give
We then receive; so 'tis Commutative.
   Oct. So great's your Friendship, you your Friend oppress;
To make it Juster, you must make it Less.
   Ant. Friendship can never err in the extent;
Like Nile, when it o'erflows, 'tis most beneficent.
   Oct. I find, Antonio, you will still subdue.
   Ant. I owe my Triumph to my Cause, not you.
Come, we lose time, your Mistress must not stay.
   Oct. Who's so accompanied, needs not fear his Way.

                       [Exeunt.

ACT THREE

(Outside) Don Henrique's house

[Camilla, Porcia, Flora appear in a balcony]

Por. Come, Cousin, the Hour assigned approaches.
Cam. Nay, more than so, for 'tis already Night.
Flo. And thanks to your Stars sufficiently dark.
Por. To the Clouds you would say, Flora, for Stars,
In this occasion, would not much befriend us.
Pray, Cousin, when Octavio shall arrive,
Do you and Flora watch above with care;
For if my cruel Brother should surprise us…
Cam. Let us alone to play the Sentinels.
Flo. I'm confident he's abroad, and will not
Suddenly return; for I heard him say,
He'd pass the Evening at the Corregidor's;
And thence, you know, he seldom comes home early.

[Enter Antonio, Octavio, and Diego, with their cloaks
over their faces, and their swords undrawn in their hands]

Ant. Is it not something early for Adventures
Of this Nature?
Oct. Tis the Hour she appointed.
Ant. How dark 'tis grown o'the sudden, there's not one
Star appears in all the Firmament.
Die. So much the better; for when I must fight,
I covet no Spectators of my Prowess.   [Aside.
Oct. Stay you here, Antonio, I'll step before,
And give the Sign, when you hear the door open,
Then come on, and follow me in.

[Enter at the other side of the stage
Henrique and Carlos]

Hen. The Corregidor's is a sweet place.
Car. The Walks and Fountains so entice me,
I still Weary myself, before I can retire.
   Hen. Indeed, we have stayed longer than we thought,
And therefore let's go home the shorter way;
The Back-door of my Garden's here at hand.
   Car. It will be better than to go about.
   Por. Would he were come, I fear the Rising Moon
Will give us little time.

[Octavio knocks upon the hilt of his sword]

I think I hear his usual knock. Who's there?
   Oct. Tis I.
   Por. I hope you're not alone.
   Oct. No; here's Diego with me, and a Friend.
   Por. Tis well; I'll open the door presently.
   Hen. Come; we are now hard by the Garden Gate.
   Oct. Let's to the door; sure she's there by this time;
Be not afraid, Diego.
   Die. You had as good command me not to breathe.
   Oct. Come on; what are you thinking on?
   Die. That I see Company, or that my Fear does.
   Oct. You're in the right; let's to avoid suspicion,
Walk on at large, till they are out of distance.

[The noise of a lock]

   Car. I think I heard your Garden door open.
   Hen. I think so too; Ha! at this time o'the night?
Why what a devil can this mean? 'Tis so.
   Ant. They have opened this door; 'tis time for me
To follow, surely Octavio is gone in.

[Antonio goes towards the door]

   Por. What stay you for?

[Holding the door half open]

   Hen. What's that I hear? sure 'tis Porcia's Voice.
   Por. What mean you to stand there? Come in I say.
   Hen. Hell and Furies!

[He goes to draw his sword]

Car. Be patient, Sir, and you will make a clearer
Discovery of your Affront.

    Por. You may come in securely, Octavio.
[Setting open the door]
I have set those will watch my Brother's coming.

    Ant. Madam, I am not Octavio.

    Por. Not Octavio? Who are you then? and who's
That shadow there?

    Hen. I can hold no longer; I'm thy Destiny,
[Draws his sword]
Vile Woman; and his Mortal Enemy.

    Ant. Ha! my Mortal Enemy?

    Hen. Yes, Villain; who e'er thou art, thou shalt pay
This Treachery with thy Life.

    Ant. Vain Man; who e'er thou art, know, the life thou
Threaten'st is guarded by a trusty sword.

[Carlos draws, and they all enter the garden fighting]

    Hen. [to Carlos] Make fast the door.
Thou art some desperate Villain hired to murder.

    Ant. [in the garden] Hired by Friendship, and Honour's my
Salary.

    Oct. That's Antonio's voice within the Garden;
[Runs to the door and finds it shut]
What! the Door shut! my Friend engaged, and I
Excluded! Cursed Fate! this Tree may help me
To climb o'er; if not, I'll fly to him.

[He climbs up]

    Die. You may do so; your sprightly Love has Wings,
And is ever Fledged; 'tis moulting time with mine;
Yet I'll up too; the hazard's not in climbing,
[Diego climbs the tree]
Here I will sit, and out of danger's reach
Expect the Issue.

The scene changes to a garden, out of which they issue fighting
(or, the garden gate opens and they re-enter fighting)

    Oct. Courage, brave Friend; you have Octavio by you.

    Ant. So seconded, a Coward would grow firm.

Hen. What! is there more of your Crew? then 'tis time
To call for help; Ho! Sylvio, Geraldo,
Pedro, come forth, and bring out Torches with you.

[Enter Sylvio with his sword drawn]

Syl. Here am I, Sir, my Comrades will follow
As soon as they have lighted their Torches.

[They fight]

Ant. How I despise these Slaves, Octavio,
Having you by me!
Die. [in the tree] Their Swords do clatter bravely in the dark.
Syl. I'm slain.

[He falls]
[Henrique stepping back, falls over Sylvio, and loses his sword,
and Carlos runs in to him]

Car. What! are you hurt?
Hen. No; I fell by chance: Help me to find my Sword.
Oct. What? D'you give back? You do well to take breath,
Whil'st you have any left; 'twill not be long,

[The rising moon appears in the scene]

Now that the Rising Moon lends us some light.

[Porcia runs out to Octavio]

Por. Oh Octavio! Let not this moment slip
To free me from my cruel Brother's Fury,
Or never hope to see me any more,
Amongst the living.

[Octavio leads her away by the arm]

Oct. Ah! Noble Maid, he that is once possessed
Of such a Treasure, and defends it not;
Let him live wretched, and detested die;
Where's my brave Friend?
Ant. You have me by your side, lead off your Mistress,
I'll secure your Retreat.
Die. [in the tree, pointing to those who are going off]
That doubtless is my Master who, victorious,
Is bravely marching off with his fair Prize;

I'll down and follow.

    Car. But whil'st I was engaged to succour you,
Our Enemies, I fear, are got away;
                  [Having helped up Henrique]
I heard the door open, and see none here;
Although the Night's much brighter than it was;
I'll follow, and trace the Villains if I can
To their Dens; meanwhile take care of your Sister;
And, pray, till my return be moderate.

    Hen. How! Moderation, in this case! what ho!
Geraldo, Pedro, ah ye cursed Rogues!

               [Enter servants with torches]

Durst ye not show your heads till they were gone?
Geraldo light me in, whil'st Pedro looks
To his hurt Companion; ah Porcia! Porcia!

               [Exit Henrique and Geraldo;
        Pedro carries out Sylvio fainting with his hurts.

        The scene changes to the city of Seville
            (or, the scene continues)

        [Enter Octavio, Porcia, Antonio,
    and a little after Diego, and after them Carlos]

    Die. [looking back at Carlos] Sure, that's Antonio bringing up
    the Rear;
Sir, they are but just before; my Master bears her
Most gallantly away; lose not sight of me.

    Car. This Rogue takes me for one of his own Crew;
He will, by his mistake, help me to harbour 'em.

                      [Exeunt.

    The scene changes to (outside) Don Henrique's house
            (or, the scene continues)

        [Camilla and Flora appear in the balcony]

    Cam. Was there ever such a Disaster, Flora?
Sure, they are all dead, so great's the silence:
Porcia, Porcia, nobody answers.

Flo. Madam, let us go down into the Garden.

Cam. Excuse me; that were to involve myself
In this unlucky scandal; 'tis possible,
Affrighted with the scuffle, she's returned
Into her Quarter by the other door;
Let's away thither.

[They go down upon the stage]
(or, they remain on the balcony)

Flo. Oh! Madam, I see a light, and Don Henrique
Coming this way with his Sword drawn, what shall
We do?

Cam. Peace; let us hide ourselves behind the door,
Till we discover his intentions.

[They go behind the door.]
(or, they exit from the balcony and reappear on ground level,
peeping round a door)

[Enter Henrique and Geraldo with a torch and Pedro with a
light, Henrique and Geraldo with their swords drawn]

Ped. Sir, I have searched all the Rooms of the House,
And cannot find her.

Hen. Base Infamous Woman; Maybe she's fled
To the Quarter ordered for Antonio.

Ped. That door is locked, and her Servant has the Key.

Hen. Ah this cursed Vagabond! thus to rob
A Brother of the Fruits of all his Care,

[He stamps]
And cast this stain on the Honour of our House,
But if ever I get the Fugitive
Within my reach, I'll sacrifice her Blood,
To the offended Spirits of my Ancestors.

Flo. Madam, d'you hear?

Cam. Yes, and tremble, Flora.

Hen. Call for her Woman.

Ped. Flora, Flora.

[Enter Flora]

Flo. My good Angel guard me; What's your pleasure
Sir?

Hen. Where's your Mistress, Hussy?
Flo. She told me, Sir, about half an hour since
She would go down into the Garden.

[Exit Flora.

Hen. My shame is certain; ah! the sad condition
Of us Men of Honour! How unequally
Our Crosses, and our Comforts mingled are!
Our Orphan Sisters are no sooner grown
Above the Follies of their Childish Age;
During which season, Custom does exact
Our Watchful Caution over all their Actions;
But they are Grafted on some stranger Stock,
Where they do Change both their Abodes and Names;
Without the least Reflection on their kindness,
Who pained themselves to cultivate their Youth,
Or else remain to exercise our fears.
O unjust Heavens! Why suffer you that they,
Who to our Joys of Life such Bubbles are,
Should add such Weight unto our Griefs, and Care?
Ah Porcia, Porcia!

[Enter Carlos]

Car. Don Henrique, if I am not much mistaken,
I have in this short time made a great Progress
Towards your Redress; I come from harbouring
The Villains, who have done you this Affront.
Cam. It imports to be attentive now.
Hen. Oh you revive me, may I but once enjoy
The Pleasure of my Revenge, though the next
Moment were the last Period of my Life,
I should depart contented; are the Villains
Within our reach?
Car. Be patient, Sir, and I'll inform you fully;
You were no sooner up, but I pursued
Your flying Enemies, hoping the night
Grown somewhat lighter, might help me to discover
The place of their Retreat; one of their Party,
Who was behind the rest, mistaking me
For one of his Comrades, bade me come on;

Saying his Master was but just before;
That he had born his Mistress bravely off,
And put her Champion Brother out of Combat.
    Hen. Insolent Rascal!

[He stamps]

    Car. We had not passed above a Street, or two,
Before he stopped, and at the second House,
Beyond the Church, in St Jago's Street,
He entered, and desired me to follow him;
I, making a Stand, he grew suspicious,
And from my silence guessing his mistake,
He slipped into the House, and locked the door;
When I had well observed the Street and House,
I came with speed, to give you this Account.
    Flo. Oh, Madam, this is Don Octavio's House;
Without all doubt, they've carried Porcia thither.
    Cam. Peace, Flora, and listen to the sequel.
    Hen. Come, Cousin; we lose time; Heigh, who
Waits there?
I will besiege the House; if they refuse
To render; I'll reduce that Theatre
Of my shame to Ashes; and make their Fort
Both Theirs, and its own Sepulchre; There are
Such Charms in Vengeance, that I do not wonder,
It is reserved for him, who formed the Thunder.
    Car. Have patience, Cousin, and consult your Reason;
'Twill soon Convince you how unpracticable
And vain your Proposition is, to attempt,
At this time of the night, a House so guarded,
In a well-governed City; that would prove
Very like Thunder, which the Cloud destroys
Wherein 'twas formed, producing only noise.
What can the Issue be, but to alarm
The Town; expose your Person and your Fortune
To the Rigour of the Law; publish your shame,
And frustrate your Revenge for ever?
    Hen. What! would you have me tarry till these Villains,
Who have invaded my House, affronted

[Spoken hastily]
My Person, murdered my Servant, and robbed
Me of a Sister, may evade my Vengeance?
   Car. No; fear not that, let me alone to find
A certain way to hinder their Escape;
I'll instantly to the Corregidor,
And beg the assistance of his Authority,
To secure these Criminals for the present;
That afterwards the Law may punish them.
   Hen. A fine Proposal! why, Cousin, can you think
That I'll submit a Personal Injury
To the tame Decision of the Formal Law?
And having been Affronted by the Sword,
To pray the Aid of the Long Robe, and take
An Advocate for Second? relieved by Law?
   Car. Since we all Parties are in making Laws,
We must not Judges be in our own Cause;
We hold it infamous to break our Words,
Yet cancel the Great Charter with our Swords.
   Hen. They by their insolence the Laws invade.
   Car. But you, by your Revenge, the Laws Degrade.
   Hen. Honour obliges me to take Revenge.
   Car. Honour is Justice, rightly understood;
Your Idol Honour's only heat of Blood.
   Hen. Honour's Opinion, which rules all the World.
   Car. Opinion, Henrique, only governs fools;
Reason the Wise, and truly Valiant rules.
   Hen. Reason's Opinion, for every one,
Stamps Reason on his own Opinion.
   Car. Then by your argument, when People join
In making Laws, because they all opine,
Laws are Reasonable, and bind us all.
   Hen. Curse on your Sophistry, to treat a Friend
With Figures, that's raging in a Fever?
You may as well pretend to teach a Man
To sing his part, that's stretched upon a Rack.
No, Sir, I'll sooner lose this irksome Life,
Than e'er consent to Publish my Disgrace,
Before I have Revenged it; To assist,

At the Funeral of my own Honour?

               [He stamps]

   Car. What a Wild Creature is a Choleric Man?   [Aside.
Tis far from my Intent; all my Design
Is only how we may Conceal your Shame,
Till we have got these Villains in our power,
Which can be brought about by no such means,
As by demanding Justice against those,
Who did assault your Person, and have wounded
Your Servant, a very plausible pretence.
Will this content you? trust my Conduct, Cousin;
Is not my Interest the same with yours?
   Hen. Well, since it must be so, I pray make haste.
   Car. Doubt not my Diligence; by this I'll prove
Friendship has Fire, and Wings as well as Love.
   Hen. If you could fly, you'ld move with too
much leisure;
Ah! tedious Minutes which Revenge does measure!

                       [Exit Carlos.

   Flo. Madam, you've heard their mischievous Design.
   Cam. Yes, Flora, out of question Porcia's there;
And if they find her, she is lost for ever.
   Flo. I'll try to hinder it, though I were certain
To perish in the Attempt; I'm confident
The House at present is in such Confusion,
I may run thither without being missed.
   Cam. Tis well thought on; in the interim
I'll retire To Porcia's Chamber.

            [Camilla exits from behind the door.

                     [Exit Henrique.

    The scene changes to inside Don Henrique's house

     [Enter Geraldo (meeting Henrique)]

   Ger. Sir, Don Antonio is just now arrived.
   Hen. Ha! what's that you say, Sirrah?

Ger. That Don Antonio, Sir, your Brother-in-law
Is without, walking i'the Hall, and bade me
Give you notice of it. Shall he come in?
    Hen. Antonio arrived! O Heavens! this Circumstance
Was only wanting to complete my Shame.
When he desires to see his Wife, shall I
My self, inform a Person of his Quality,
That she is run away? where shall I find
A Heart, a Tongue, a Voice, or Breath, or Face,
To utter this unparalleled Disgrace?
Oh this fantastic sense of Honour! I
At my own Tribunal stand assoiled,
Yet fearing others' Censure am embroiled.
    Ger. What is your pleasure, Sir; 'tis possible
That Don Antonio may think it long.
    Hen. Wait on him in, but at the same time tell him,
You cannot find me; I will leave my House,
And the Discovery of my shame to Fate;
And any Censure rather undergo,
Than be the Reporter of my own Disgrace;
Till first I have my Honour's Ransom paid,
In the Vile Blood of this Perfidious Maid.

                              [Exit Henrique.

              [Enter Antonio and Ernesto]

    Ant. My Friend and his fair Mistress safely Lodged,
And free from their Adventure; 'Tis now fit
To mind my own Engagement; But, Ernesto,
What can the meaning be of this Rude usage?
In suffering me to stay without thus long,
Upon my first Arrival? Come, let's go on
Into the other Rooms.
    Ern. I swear, Sir, I'm amazed at this great Change;
Tis not above two hours, since I found here
A numerous, and well ordered Family,
In all appearance; now I see the Pages
Bolt out of the Doors, then start back again
Into their holes, like Rabbits in a Warren;
The Maids lie peeping at the Garret windows,

Like the Upper Tier of Ordnance in a Ship;
All looks disordered now; nor can I guess
What may have caused so strange an Alteration;
But there I see the Servant you sent in.

[Enter Geraldo]

Ant. Friend, Where's your Master?
Ger. I cannot tell, Sir.
Ant. Where is his Sister?
Ger. In truth I know not, Sir; we Men-servants
Have little to do in the Ladies' Quarters.

[Exit Geraldo.

Ant. This looks but oddly; are you sure Ernesto,
You've not misguided me to a wrong House?
Ern. If you are sure, Sir, that we are awake,
Then I am certain this is the same House,
Wherein this Afternoon, I saw, and spoke with
Don Henrique, and your Bride; by the same Token
There was a Lady with her in a Veil;
And this very Room is the Ante-Chamber
To her Apartment.
Ant. I should be finely served, if after all
This Negotiation, and a tedious Journey,
My Pains, and Patience should be cast away
On some such withered Sybil, for a Wife,
As her own Brother is ashamed to show me.
Ern. You'll soon be freed from that fear, Sir.

[Ernesto goes towards the door]

Ant. How so?
Ern Because I see her in the Inner Room,
Lying along upon her Couch, and Reading;
Her Face is turned the other way, but yet
Her Shape, and Clothes assure me 'tis the same.
Ant. Art certain that 'tis she?
Ern. There are not many like her.
Ant. If thou be sure 'tis she, I'll venture in,
Without her Brother's Presence to introduce me.
Ern. She's coming this way, Sir.

[Enter Camilla reading]

Cam. You have reason, Dido, and 'tis well Remarked,
      [She shuts her book, after a little pause]
The Woman, who suffers herself to love,
Ought likewise to prepare herself to suffer;
There was great Power in your Charms, Aineas,
To enthral a Lady's heart at first approach,
And make such early, and such deep Impressions,
That nothing, but her Death, could ere deface.
Alas! poor Dido...
    Ant. O Heavens! What's that I see; or do I Dream?
      [Antonio seeing her, starts, then stands as if amazed]
Sure I am asleep; and 'tis a Vision
Of her, who's always present to my Thoughts;
Who fearing my Revolt, does now Appear
To Prove, and to confirm my Constancy.
When first I saw that Miracle, she seemed
An Apparition. Here it must be one.
    Ern. What fit of Frenzy's this? Sir, 'tis Porcia,
A Lovely Living Woman, and your Bride.
    Ant. The Blessing is too mighty for my Faith.
    Ern. Faith! Ne'er trouble your Faith, in this Occasion,
Approach her boldly, Sir, and trust your sense.
    Ant. As when we Dream of some Transporting Pleasure,
And finding that we Dream, we fear to Wake,
Least Sense should rob us of our Fancy's Treasure,
And our Delightful Vision from us take;
Blessed Apparition, so it fares with me.
That very Angel, now, once more appears,
To whose Divinity, long since, I raised
An Altar in my heart; where I have offered
The constant Sacrifice of Sighs, and Vows.
My eyes are open! yet I dare not trust 'em;
Bliss above Faith must pass for an Illusion;
If such it be, O let me sleep for ever
Happily deceived; but Celestial Maid,
If this thy glorious Presence Real be,
Oh let one word of Pity raise my Soul
From Visionary bliss, and make me die

With real Joy instead of Extasy.
Speak, speak, my Destiny, for the same breath
May warm my Heart, or cool it into Death.
    Ern 'Slife! he's in one of his old Fits again;
Why what d'you mean, Sir? 'tis Porcia herself.
    Cam. I am that Maid, who to your Virtue owes
Her Honour then, and her Disquiet since;
Yet in my Pain, I cannot but be pleased
To find a Passion, censured in our Sex,
Justified, by so great an Obligation.
Tis true, I blush, yet I must own the Fire,
To which both Love, and Gratitude conspire.
    Ant. Incomparable Creature! can it be?
That having suffered all, which mighty Love
Did e'er inflict, I now should be Repaid
With as full Joys, as Love could ever give;
Fortune, to make my Happiness complete,
Has joined her Power, and made me find a Bride
In a Lost Mistress, but with this Allay,
Of leaving me no means my Faith to prove,
Since Chance anticipates the Pains of Love.
    Cam. The Servant's Error has misled the Master,
He takes me too for Porcia, blessed Mistake;
Assist me now, Artful Dissimulation;   [Aside.
But how can that consist with so much Passion?
Tis possible, the sense of my distressed
Condition, might dispose a noble heart
To take Impressions then, which afterwards
Time, and your Second Thoughts may have defaced;
But can a Constant Passion be produced
From those Ideas, Pity introduced?
Let your Tongue speak your Heart, for should you
    abuse me,
I shall in time discover the Deceit;
You may paint Fire, Antonio, but not Heat.
    Ant. Madam.
    Cam. Hold; be not too scrupulous, Antonio;
Let me Believe it, though it be not True;
For the chief Happiness poor Maids receive,
Is, when themselves they happily deceive.

Ant. If, since those Conquering Eyes I first beheld,
You have not reigned Unrivalled in my Heart;
May you Despise me, now you are my own,
Which is to me, all Curses summed in one.
But, may your Servant, Madam, take the boldness
To ask, if you have ever Thought of Him?
    Cam. A Love, so founded in a grateful Heart,
Has need of no Remembrancer, Antonio;
You know yourself too well; those of your Trade
Have skill to Hold, as well as to Invade.
    Ant. Fortune has lifted me to such a Height
Of Happiness, that it may Turn my Brain,
When I look down upon the lower world.
What have I now to wish but Moderation
To Temper, and to fix my Joys?
    Cam. I yield as little to you, noble Antonio,
In Happiness, as Affection, but still
Porcia must do as may become your Bride,
And Sister to Don Henrique; in whose absence
A longer Conference must be excused.
Therefore I take the freedom to withdraw.
Should I have stayed until Don Henrique came,
His presence would have marred my whole design.

[Aside; exit Camilla.

    Ant. Where Beauty, Virtue, and Discretion join,
Tis Heaven, methinks, to find that Treasure mine.

[Enter Henrique]

    Hen. Sure, Don Antonio, having long ere this
Found out the infamous flight of my vile Sister,
Will be retired to meditate Revenge
Upon us both.
[He sees him]
Ah Curse! he is there still;
I'll slip away–But it is now too late,
He has perceived me.
    Ant. How, Don Henrique! Avoid your Friend
    that's come
So long a Journey to embrace you, and cast

Himself at the feet of your fair Sister?

Hen. Noble Antonio, you may well Imagine
The trouble I am in, that you should find
My House in such Disorder, so unfit
To receive the Honour of so brave a Guest.

Ant. Tis true, Don Henrique, I am much surprised
With what I find; I little did expect
Your Sister Porcia should have been–

Hen. Oh Heavens! I'm lost, he has discovered all.   [Aside.
Tis not, Antonio, in a Brother's power
To make a Sister of a better Paste,
Than Heaven has made her.

Ant. In your case specially; for, without doubt,
Heaven never made a more Accomplished Creature.

Hen. What means the Man?

Ant. I come just now from Entertaining her:
Whose wit, and beauty so excel all those
Of her fair Sex whom I have ever known,
That my Description of her would appear
Rather Detraction, than a just Report
Of her Perfections.

Hen. Certainly he mocks me; he never could
Have chosen a worse Sufferer of Scorn;
But I will yet contain myself a while,
To see how far he'll drive it.   [Aside.
Say you, Sir,
That you have Seen, and Entertained my Sister?

Ant. Yes, Don Henrique; and with such full
     Contentment,
So raised above Expression, that I think
The Pains, and Care of all my former life
Rewarded with Excess, in the Delight
Of those few Minutes of her Conversation;
Tis true, that satisfaction was abridged
By her well-weighed Severity; to give me
A greater Pleasure, in the Contemplation
Of her discreet Observance of the Rules
Of Decency; not suffering me, though now
Her Husband, any longer to enjoy
So great a Happiness, you not being by.

Hen. I am confounded; but I must dissemble
My Astonishment, till I can unfold
The Mystery; She might have spared that Caution,   [Aside.
But I suppose you'll easily forgive
An Error on the Better side.

 Ant. Sir, I have seen so much of her Perfection
In that short Visit, I shall sooner doubt
Our Definitions in Morality,
Than once suppose her capable of Error.

 Hen. This Exposition makes it more Obscure:
I must get him away. Sir; Is it not time   [Aside.
To wait on you to your Chambers? It's late,
And I believe that you have need of rest.

 Ant. I should accept your offer, Sir, with thanks,
If I were not obliged, as late as 'tis
To see a Friend before I go to Bed.

 Hen. I'll bear you company, if you'll give me leave.

 Ant. I humbly thank you, Sir, but can't consent
To give you so much trouble; I'll return
Within an hour at farthest.

 Hen. Whene'er you please; you are wholly
Master here.

 Ant. I never saw a Man so Discomposed,
Whate'er the matter is.   [Aside.
Ernesto, I must make a step to see
A Friend near hand; bid Sancho follow me;
And stay you in my Chamber till I come.

       [Exit Antonio, Ernesto.

Hen. Your servant, Sir.

    [Henrique waits on him to the door]

This sudden Sally hence
At this time of the night, newly arrived
From a Long Journey, and not to suffer me
To wait upon him, does embroil me more.
But now I will not long be in suspense;
I'll to my Sister's Chamber.

[Enter Carlos as Henrique is going into Porcia's chamber]

Car. Ho! Don Henrique, come away, all's Prepared,
Our Kinsman the Corregidor is ready
With a strong Band of Sergeants; and stays for you.
Hen. Speak softly; Don Antonio is arrived.
And some of his may overhear us.
Car. That's very unlucky, but does he know
Your Sister's Missing?
Hen. I think not yet.
Car. Come, let's away; we have no time to lose.
Hen. Pray stay a while; I labour with a doubt
Will burst me, if not cleared before I go.
Car. What Cousin! Will you lose an opportunity
Never to be recovered? Are you Mad?
Will you permit the Villains to escape,
And laugh at us for ever? Come away.

[He pulls him]

Hen. Well, I must go; and let time make it out;
The worst Estate of Human Life is Doubt.

[Exeunt.

ACT FOUR

(A room in) Don Octavio's house

[Enter Octavio angrily pushing Diego, and Porcia following]

Oct. Villain, thou hast undone us; cursed Villain;
Where was thy Soul? Had fear quite banished it,
And left thee not one grain of Common sense?
    Por. Was there ever so fatal an Accident?
    Oct. Why Traitor, Did'st thou not let me know it,
As soon as we were come into the House?
    Die. What would you have done if you'd known it then?
    Oct. I would have Sallied out, and killed the Rogue,
In whose Power thou hast put it to destroy us;
Can it be doubted, but that long ere this
He has acquainted Henrique where we are?
From whose black Rage we must immediately
Expect to encounter all the worst extremes
Of malice, seconded by seeming Justice;
For the Unfortunate are still i'the wrong.
Curse on all Cowards! better far be served
By Fools, and Knaves: they make less dangerous faults.
    Die. Am I in fault, because I'm not a Cat?
How could I tell i'the dark whether that Rascal
Were a Knight Errant, or a Recreant Knight?
I thought him one of us, and true to Love;
Were it not for such Accidents as these
That mock Man's Forecast, sure the Destinies
Had ne'er been placed amongst the Deities.
    Oct. Peace, cowardly Slave; having thus played the Rogue,
Are you grown Sententious? Did I not Fear
To stain my Sword with such Base Blood, I'd let
Thy Soul out with it at a thousand Wounds.
    Die. Why then a thousand Thanks to my Base Blood,

For saving my Good Flesh. [Aside.
Oct. Pardon, my dearest Mistress, this Excess
Of Passion in your Presence.
Por. What shall we do Octavio if we stay here,
We are undone for ever: my Brother
Will be instantly upon us. Alas!
My own Life I value not Octavio,
When yours, my Better life, such hazard runs;
But Oh my Honour! Oh my Innocence!
Exposed to Scandal; there's my deepest sense.
Oct. Though the Complexion of your Brother's Malice
Resemble Hell, it is not Black enough
To cast a stain upon your Virgin Innocence.
Sure two such different branches ne'er did spring
From the same stock; To me it seems very strange;
Our middle Natures formed of Flesh and Blood,
Should have such depths of Ill, such heights of Good;
An Angel Sister, and a Devil Brother.
Por. He's my Brother, and I know no defence
For injured Innocence, but Innocence.
Fly, fly, Octavio, leave me to my fate.
Oct. Your kindness, Generous Maid, confutes itself.
To save my life, you Counsel me to fly,
Which is at once to bid me live, and die.
Por. What then, for Heaven's sake do you resolve to do?
Oct. I must resolve, and suddenly, but what, I swear
I know not, there have been such Turns
In my Misfortunes, they have made me giddy.
Por. You must determine; time wastes, Octavio.
Oct. Madam, if I should lead you through the Streets,
And chance to meet the Officers of Justice,
I not daring to avow my Person,
For that unlucky Accident you know of,
You might, I fear, by that means, be in danger,
We must not venture it; Run, Rascal, and fetch
A Chair immediately.
Die. A pretty Errand at this time o'the night;
These Chairmen are exceedingly well natured,
They're likely to obey a Servant's orders
After nine a'Clock. [Exit Diego.

Oct. Ye Powers above, why do ye lay so great
A weight on Human Nature, and bestow
Such an unequal Force to bear our Loads?
After a long Pursuit, through all those Storms,
Which Hellbred Malice, or the Power of Fate
Could ever raise, to oppress a Noble Love;
To be at length possessed of the Rich Mine,
Where Nature seemed to have lodged all her Treasure;
And in an Instant have it Ravished from me,
   Oct. Where is it?
   Die. Even where it was; they are deeply engaged
At Las Pintas, and will not leave their Game,
They swear, for all the Dons in Seville.
   Oct. A curse upon these Rogues! I'll make 'em come,
Or make their hearts ache.

[Octavio runs out]

   Die. Madam, though I was never yet Unkind
To my own Person, I am so much troubled
At the Disquiet my mistake has brought you,
That could I do it conveniently, i'Faith,
I would even cudgel myself.
   Por. Away Buffoon, Is this a time for fooling?

[Enter Antonio and Sancho]

   Ant. Where is my noble Friend Octavio?
   Die. Did you not meet him at the Door, Sir?
   Ant. No.
   Die. He went out, Sir, just as you came in.
   Ant. Madam, I might have gone to Bed, but not
To Rest, without returning to enquire
Of yours, and of my noble Friend's condition;
And once more to offer you my Service.
   Por. I take the boldness in Octavio's absence
To return his, with my most humble Thanks,
For your late generous Assistance of us;
And for this new Addition to our Debt.
   Ant. Though I have not the honour to be known to you,
The Service of your Sex, in their Distresses,
Is the first vow of those of our Profession;

And my constant friendship for Octavio
Is of so old a Date, that all occasions,
By which I may express the fervour of it,
Are most welcome to me.

            [Enter Flora in great haste]

    Flo. Oh Madam I'm out of breath with running.
    Por. What accident Flora brings you hither?
    Flo. A sad one, Madam, and requiring haste,
To give you timely notice on't; Don Carlos
Assisted by the light o'the rising Moon,
And by a mistake of some of your Train,
Has traced you to this House, and in my hearing,
Informed your Brother of the Place, and Manner
Of your Retreat; who is now coming hither
Accompanied with the Corregidor,
To seize on whomsoever shall be found
Within these Walls, upon pretence of Murder.
    Por. Oh cruel Accident!
    Flo. Madam, make haste, get out at the back door;
Or you will certainly be met with.
    Por. How vile a Creature am I now become!
For though in my own Innocence secure,
To the censorious World, who like false Glasses
Mingling their own irregular Figures,
Misreflect the Object, I shall appear
Some sinful Woman, sold to Infamy.
    Ant. Your own clear mind's the Glass, which to yourself
Reflects yourself; and trust me, Madam,
We are only happy then, when all our joys,
Flow from ourselves, not from the People's voice.
    Flo. Madam, They'll instantly be here.
    Por. Oh that Octavio should just now be absent!
But to expect till he return were Madness.
    Ant. You have Reason, Madam, and if you dare trust
Your Person to the Conduct of a Stranger,
Upon my Honour, Lady, I'll secure you,
Or perish in the Attempt.
    Por. Generous Sir, How shall a wretched Maid,
Abandoned by her Fate to the pursuit

Of an Inhumane Brother, e'er be able
Either to merit, or Requite your Favours?
   Ant. I am the Obliged, if rightly understood,
Being o'er-paid by the joy of doing good.
   Por. Sir, I Resign myself to your Protection,
With equal Gratitude, and Confidence.
   Ant. Come Madam, we must lose no time;
Diego, find out your Master presently,
And tell him, That the Danger not allowing
Our stay till his Return, I shall convey
His Mistress safely to a Nunnery.

[Exit Diego.

   Por. And Flora, stay you here to bring me word,
What he Resolves to do in this our desperate
Condition.
   Flo. Madam, I shall.

[Antonio goes but returns]

   Ant. But stay; I swear, I'd like to have committed.
A foul mistake; the Monastery Gates
Will not be opened at this time o'the night,
Without a strict Inquiry into the Cause;
Besides, 'tis possible, that once lodged there,
She may be out of my Friend's Power, or mine,
Ever to get her thence, if it be known.
It must not be. [He pauses and thinks]
I have thought better on't;
I will convey you to my Brother-in-Law's,
A person of such Quality and Honour,
As may protect and serve you with his Credit:
And there my Wife may have the happiness
To accompany you; and pay the Offices
Due to your Virtue and distressed Condition:
And going to a House that's so much mine,
Make account, Madam, 'tis to your own Home.
[Turning to Sancho]
Sancho, Stay you here, to attend Octavio,
And guide him the next way to my Apartment;
Here is the Key; I shall have little use on't,

Having Ernesto waiting for me there.
One word more, Sancho, Let Octavio know
Tis my advice, that he come in a Chair;
He by that means may possibly escape
Examination, if he should be met with.
    Por. Flora, I pray do you continue here,
And if by any accident, Octavio
Should be hindered from coming after us,
Observe his motions well, and where he fixes;
Then return home, and I shall find some way
Of sending to you, to inform myself
    Flo. I shall not fail to observe your Orders, Madam.
    Ant. Madam, I am ready to attend you.
    Por. Ah cruel Brother! Ah my dear Octavio!
How am I tortured betwixt Love and Hate!
    Ant. We had better Suffer, than Deserve our Fate.

                    [Exit Antonio, Porcia.

    San. Tis no small Compliment my Master makes
Your Lady, and her Gallant, at this time
O'the night to quit his Brother-in-Law's, and leave
So fair a Bride as Porcia all alone.
    Flo. What, is his Mistress's Name Porcia too?
    San. Yes; and if she has as fair a Handmaid
As yourself, I shall soon forget my Damsels
In the Low Counries.
    Flo. If your Low Country Damsels resemble us,
You would not be put to it to forget first.
But I believe that you are safe enough;
I have not heard such praises of their wit,
But that we may suppose they have good memories.

              [Enter Diego]

    Die. Is not my Master yet returned?
    Flo. No.
    Die. Well; now have we an Honourable Cause
To wear the Beadle's Livery; faith, Flora,
If your tender Sex had not been privileged
From this harsh Discipline, how prettily
Would the Beadle's Crimson Lace show upon

Your white back.

Flo. 'Twon't do so well as on a darker ground;
'Twill suit much better with your Tawny hide.

San. I pray, Comrade, is it the Mode in Seville
To be whipped for Company?

Die. Oh Sir, a well-bred Soldier will ne'er refuse
Such a Civility to an old friend;
This is a new way of being a Second,
To show your Passive Courage.

San. We Soldiers do not use to show our Backs.

Die. Not to your Enemies; but, Sir, the Beadle
Will prove your Friend, for your Blood being heated
With Riding Post, the Breathing of a Vein
Is very requisite.

San. Would to Heaven that I were i'the Camp again,
There we are never stripped till we are Dead.

[Enter Octavio, and the chair-men appear at the door]

Oct. Be sure you stir not thence till I return.
                    [To the chair-men]
Sirrah, where's Porcia?

Die. She's fled away i'the dark, with a young man
Of your Acquaintance.

Oct. Rascal, leave your fooling.

Die. There's none i'the case, Sir, 'tis the wisest thing
She ever did, had she stayed your return,
She would have fallen into those very Clutches,
In which you will immediately be gripped,
Unless you make more haste; Flora is come
With all the speed she could, to let you know
They're coming with the Justice, to lay hold
Of all within this House; pray be quick, Sir,
And save yourself. She's safe in a Nunnery;
Conducted thither by Antonio.

Oct. Peace Screech Owl; Fire consume that Tongue of
   thine.
What say'st thou Villain? in a Nunnery?
Porcia in a Nunnery? Oh Heavens! nothing
But this was wanting to make me desperate;
What hope's there left ever to get her thence,

After such Accidents as these made public?
Ah Flora, is it true, that my dear Porcia
Is gone into a Nunnery?
   Flo. Once, Sir, 'twas so resolved, and Diego sent
To give you notice on't; but afterwards,
He being gone, they changed their Resolutions:
There's one can tell you more. [Pointing to Sancho]
   San. My Master bade me stay, to let you know
He has conveyed her to his own Apartment,
In his Brother-in-Law's House, a Person
So eminent in Quality and Credit,
That the Engaging him in her, and your
Protection, Sir, may much avail ye both;
Besides, she'll have the satisfaction there
Of being treated by my Master's Bride.
There he'll Expect you, and Advises you
To come in a Chair, to avoid Questioning,
In case of any Encounter.
   Oct. I'll take his Counsel, he's a generous Friend,
Come Chairmen away.
[To Sancho] Pray Friend, do you guide us.
   Die. Up with your Burden Beasts, and fall forth-with
To your Half Trot.

                                      [Exeunt.

The scene changes to a street

[The chair is carried on to the stage.
Diego, Sancho and Flora follow]

   Car. (within) Follow, follow, follow.

[Enter Carlos, the corrregidor and sergeants,
pursuing Sancho, Flora, and Diego]

   Die. This is one of Don Cupid's pretty Jests.
We're struck upon a shelf before we could
Put out to Sea.
   Car. You find, Sir, my Conjectures not ill grounded.

[To the corregidor]

Cor. What are you Sirrah?
Die. A living Creature, very like a man.
Only I want a Heart.
    Cor. You're pleasant, Sir, pray Heaven your
mirth continue.
Who is that Woman with the Veil?
    Die. Let her answer for herself, she has a Tongue,
Set it but once a'going, and she'll tell
All that she knows and more.
    Cor. Make her uncover her face.

        [One of the sergeants goes to lift up her veil]

    Car. Hold Friend; Cousin, if it should be Porcia,
[Turning to the corregidor] It were not fit to expose
her here.
    Cor. Tis very well considered; go you to her,
And speak to her in private.

        [Carlos goes towards Flora]

    Flo. Tis I Sir, Flora, who being commanded
By my Lady...
    Car. Speak softly, prithee Flora, 'tis enough;
I understand the rest, and pity her;
Bid her sit still i'the Chair, I'll do my best
To save her from dishonour.
    Flo. He thinks 'tis Porcia there, a good mistake;
It may secure Octavio from the hands
Of this rude Rabble.   [Aside.
They take you for my Mistress, Sir, sit still.
        [To Octavio in the chair]
I'll follow the Chair, and watch all Occasions
To further your Escape.
    Car. We have found our Wandering Nymph, Sir.
    Cor. Was it Porcia?
    Car. No, Sir, 'twas her Waiting woman, Flora,
Following the Chair; wherein they were conveying
Her Lady to some other Place.
    Cor. We arrived luckily, had we but stayed,
A moment longer, they had all been fled.
    Ser. Will you have us see, Sir, who's i'the Chair?

Cor. Forbear Fellow!
[To Carlos] Her own folly is punishment enough
To a Woman of her Quality, without
Our adding that of Public Shame.
        Car. 'Twas happily thought on, when you obliged
Don Henrique to expect us at your House;
For had he come, and found his sister here,
It had been impossible to have restrained
His Passion from some great Extravagance.
        Cor. I could not think it fit to let him come;
For one of such a Spirit would ne'er brook
The sight of those had done him these Affronts.
Tis better that a business of this Nature,
Especially 'twixt Persons of such Quality,
Should be composed, if it were possible,
By the Mediation of some chosen Friends,
Than brought to a public Trial of the Law;
Or, which is worse, some Barbarous Revenge.
        Car. This Fellow (if I am not much mistaken)
                [Looking upon Diego]
Is Don Octavio's Man.
        Cor. Who do you belong to, Friend?
        Die. To nobody, Sir.
        Cor. Do not you serve?
        Die. Yes Sir, but my Master is not himself.
        Cor. Take his Sword from him, Sergeant.

        [The sergeant goes to take away his sword]

Die. Diego disarmed? By any other hand
Than by his own? Know Friend, it is a Weapon
Of such dire Execution, that I dare not
Give it up, but to the hands of Justice.

        [The corregidor receives the sword, and gives it
                to one of his sergeants]

Pray call for it Sir, as soon as you come home,
And hang it up in your Hall, then under-write,
This is bold Diego's Sword; Oh may it be
Ever from Rust, as 'tis from Slaughter free.
        Cor. Thou art a Fellow of a pleasant Humour.

Die. Faith Sir, I never pain myself for Love,
Or Fame, or Riches; nor do I pretend
To that great Subtlety of Sense, to Feel
Before I am hurt; and for the most part.
I keep myself out of Harm's way.
    Car. The Definition of a Philosopher.
    Cor. Come, leave your fooling, Sirrah, where's your
Master?
    Die. The only way to leave my fooling Sir
Is to leave my Master; for without doubt
Whoever has but the least grain of Wit,
Would never serve a Lover Militant;
He had better wait upon a Mountebank,
And be run through the Body twice a Week,
To recommend his Balsam.
    Cor. This Fellow's an Original.
    Die. But of so ill a hand, I am not worth
The hanging up, Sir, in my Master's room,
Amongst the worst of your Collection.

[Enter sergeants with two footmen and two maidservants]

    Ser. An't please your Worship, we have searched the House,
From the Cellars to the Garrets, and these
Are all the living Cattle we can find.
    Cor. Friends, take a special care of that same Varlet,
And the Waiting-woman; we'll find a way
To make them tell the Truth, I warrant you.
    Flo. Oh Diego! must we be Prisoners together?
    Die. Why, that's not so bad as the Bands of Wedlock, Flora.
    Cor. Come, let's away; but whether to convey her
To her own House, certainly were not fit,
Because of her incensed Brother.
    Car. If you approve on't, Cousin, I'll carry her
To mine; for since we seek (if possible)
To compose the Business, she will be there
With much more decency and satisfaction;
Being in a Kinsman's House, and where she'll have
My Sister to accompany her.
    Cor. This Business cannot be in better Hands,
Than yours; and there I'll leave it, and bid you Goodnight.

Car. Your Servant, Cousin, I wish you well at home.
You may be pleased to take your Sergeants with you.
　　　　[As the corregidor goes out]
There are without two Servants of Don Henrique's.
They'll be enough to guard our Prisoners,
And with less notice.
　　Cor. Come, Sergeants, follow me.
　　Car. Well, ye may go about your business, Friends,
　　　　[To the footmen and maids]
I'm glad we did not find Octavio here;
For though I might justly pretend Ignorance,
I would not have him suffer, though by chance.

　　　　　　　　　　　　　[Exit servants.

San. Well, I am now sufficiently instructed,
And since there is no notice taken of me,
I'll fairly steal away, and give my Master,
An Account of this Misfortune.

　　　　　　　　　　　　　[Exit Sancho.

　　Car. Take up the Chair and follow me.

　　　　[They take up the chair]

　　Die. A Lovely Dame they bear; 'tis true, she's something
Hairy about the Chin, but that, they say's,
A Sign of Strength: It tickles me to think
How like an Ass he'll look, when opening the Shell,
His Worship finds within so rough a Kernel.

　　　　　　　　　　　　　[Exeunt.

　　The scene changes to Don Antonio's apartment
　　　　in Don Henrique's House.

　　　　[Enter Antonio and Porcia]

　　Ant. Madam, Banish your fear, you are now safe
Within these Walls; be pleased to remain here,
Till I shall bring some Lights, and acquaint Porcia
With the Honour she'll receive in entertaining

So fair a Guest.
   Por. Who is't, you say, you will advertise, Sir?
   Ant. My Wife Porcia; Have but a little patience,
And she'll attend you Madam.

                                    [Exit Antonio.

   Por. Is her Name Porcia too? Pray Heaven send her
A better Fate than her distressed Namesake.
But whither am I brought? What House is this?
What with my fears, and darkness of the Night,
I have lost all my Measures, I can't guess
What Quarter of the Town it is we're in,
For to avoid the meeting with my Brother,
And his Revengeful Train, we have been forced
To make so many Turnings, I am giddy.
But, thanks to Providence, I have this comfort,
That, now, I'm in a Place out of his reach.

   [Enter Antonio with two lights, and sets them on the table]

   Ant. Madam, My Wife will suddenly attend you.
Pardon, I pray, my absence for a moment.

                                      [Exit Antonio.

   Por. Now I begin to hope my Sighs and Tears,
Have in some measure with just Heaven prevailed
At length to free me... But what do I see!
                [Looking about her, she starts]
Am I awake, or is it an Illusion?
Bless me, is not this my Brother's House? this
The Quarter joining to my own Apartment?
There is no room for doubt, and my Misfortunes
Are always certain, and without redress.
Unerring Powers, Arbiters of Fate,
Teach me my Crimes, and how to expiate
Your wrath: Alas, I know not what I've done,
To merit this continued Persecution?
But how came I here? brought by Octavio's Friend,
One, on whose Virtue, I did so rely,
That I my Brother's Malice durst defy.
Can he betray me? sure I'm in a Dream.

But if Octavio... Oh vile suspicion!
Octavio false? No, Truth and he are one.
Tis possible his Friend may guilty be;
But to what end so base a Treachery:
And if Perfidious, how could he be his Friend?
I am confounded with the various forms
Of my Misfortunes, heightened still the more,
The less I can their Hidden Cause explore.
This only's evident, that I must fly
Immediately this Fatal Place; But why
Struggle I thus with Fate? since go, or stay,
              [She weeps]
Death seems alike to wait me every way.

      [Enter Antonio and Camilla]

  Cam. I wonder much what Lady this can be
Antonio mentions.   [Aside.
  Ant. Pardon, I beseech you Madam, the liberty
Which I so early take; but I presume
Such is your Generous Tenderness to those,
Whose spiteful Fortunes, not their Fault, has brought
Into Distress, that you will think yourself
Obliged to him, who gives you the occasion
To exercise those Virtues, which only visit
Others, but reside with you; This fair Lady...
But she will best relate her own sad Story;
Whil'st I seek out Don Henrique, and engage him
To employ his Power and Interest for her service.

                 [Exit Antonio.

      [Upon Camilla's approach
Porcia takes the handkerchief from her eyes]

  Cam. Ha! what's that I see? Stay, stay Antonio.
        [She runs after Antonio]
It is not fit Don Henrique... but he's gone,
And we are lost for ever.
  Por. O Heavens! Is this Antonio, the same Man
To whom I am Betrothed? then my Destruction

Is inevitable.

Cam. Are you an Apparition? or are you
Porcia herself? speak; that when you've said it thrice
I may not yet believe you.

Por. You well may doubt, even what you see, Camilla;
Since my Disasters are so new, and strange,
They sever Truth from Credibility.

Cam. How is it possible you should be here?

Por. I know not how; only of this I'm sure,
I have not long to expect the dismal end
Of my sad Tragedy; since 'tis evident,
The Person, that hath led me to this Place,
This fatal Place, is the abused Antonio;
Who has conspired with my unnatural Brother,
To take away my wretched life, and chose
This Scene, as fittest for their Cruelty.
And thus, strange Fate! (through Ignorance betrayed)
I have sought Protection from the same Party,
Whom I have injured; and have made my Husband
The only Confidant of his own Affront:
Who to accomplish his too just Revenge,
As well upon my Family, as Person,
Gives me up to be murdered by my Brother.
So, whil'st I'm branded as a Faithless Bride,
He'll be detested, as a Parricide.

Cam. Prodigious Accident! but wert thou blind
Not to know thine own House, unhappy Porcia?

Por. Alas, how could I? in so dark a Night,
In such Confusion, and so full of fear?
Besides, he brought me in by the Back-way,
Through his own Quarter, where was neither Light,
Nor any Creature of the Family.

Cam. Although I cannot comprehend the steps
Of this your strange Adventure, yet dear Cousin,
Your case (as I conceive) is not so desperate.

Por. We easily persuade ourselves to hope
The things we wish.
But Cousin, my condition
Will not admit self-flattery, and what
Can you propose to temper my Despair?

Cam. Don't you remember, how this Afternoon
Antonio's man finding me in your Quarter
Without a Veil (you having put on mine)
That he applied himself to me, and I,
By your command, assumed your Person.
    Por. Yes very well.
    Cam. The Master since has by the Man's mistake
Been happily led into the same Error.
I have not disabused him yet, in hopes
It might produce Advantage to us both.
    Por. Oh! he has spoken with my Brother since,
Who sure has undeceived him long ere this.
No, without doubt, they having found themselves
Affronted both, have both conspired my death.
    Cam. How Cousin can that be? if Don Antonio
Has engaged himself, in your Protection,
And is Octavio's Friend.
    Por. Cousin, If you impartially reflect
On the Affront which I have done Antonio,
You will not wonder much, if he recede
From the scarce trodden Path of rigid Honour,
To meet with his Revenge; and to that end
Proceeds thus cautelously; still pretending
He knows not me; that he may disavow
Both to Octavio and to all the world
The Infamy of Betraying a poor Maid
To loss of Life and Honour.
    Cam. Misfortunes make you rave; this vile Suspicion
Is inconsistent with Antonio's Fame;
                [Spoken with heat]
You may as well believe, that Nature will
Reverse the Order of the whole Creation
As that Antonio, a Man, whose Soul
Is of so strong and perfect a Complexion,
Should e'er descend to such a slavish sin.
And if we had the leisure, I could give you
Such Reasons to convince you of your Error,
That you would both acknowledge and repent it.
    Por. Alas! I had forgot her near Concernments   [Aside.
For Antonio. Pardon and pity me Camilla;

My mind is so distracted by Afflictions,
I know not what I should, or should not Fear;
 Cam. I pity thee with all my heart; but Cousin,
If Antonio, not knowing you, nor your
Relations, should chance to find your Brother,
And tell him unawares all that has passed,
And that he has brought the distressed Party hither;
He'll presently imagine it is you;
And then (I fear) 'twill be impossible
(Though he should interpose with all his power)
To stop the Torrent, or divert his Rage
From breaking in, and executing on us
That horrid Parricide, which (though too late)
It may be he himself would execrate.
 Por. There's too much ground for what you fear, Camilla;
But if I could secure myself this night,
Tis very possible, that tomorrow
We might engage Antonio and your Brother
To find out some Expedient to relieve me.
 Cam. Were you only in pain for your security
This night, I know an easy Remedy
For that.
 Por. Which way, my Dearest?
 Cam. Why what does hinder us from making use
(On this occasion) of the secret door,
By which (you know) you have so often passed
Into our House, upon more pleasing Errands?
By this we shall obtain these benefits
Of safety from your Brother's present Fury,
And time to try if Carlos and Antonio
May be engaged to mediate in this Business.
And I have cause to think you will not find
Antonio so implacable as you
Imagine.
 Por. I conceive you Cousin, Fool that I was,
To think a Heart once conquered by your Eyes,
Should e'er become another Virgin's Prize.

[Enter Antonio]

 Ant. So late! a Guest in's House! that's come so far!

On such a Business! and not yet come home?
There's something in't I cannot comprehend.   [Aside.
Madam, I haven't as yet found out your Brother,
But sure 'twill not be long, ere he return.
Then I'll acquaint him with the Accident
Has made his House this Lady's Sanctuary.
   Por. Here is a Glimpse of Comfort, for I see
He takes my Cousin for Don Henrique's Sister;
O blessed mistake, so luckily continued!   [Aside.
   Cam. I am by his permission Mistress here,
And since that I am pleased Sir, 'tis enough,
Without our troubling him with the Account
Of her sad Story.
   Ant. True, Madam, as to her Reception here,
But yet 'twere very fit he knew it too,
That we might serve ourselves of his Advice,
And Credit for this Lady's service.

          [Enter Henrique]

   Hen. Though I did promise the Corregidor
Not to stir from his House till his return,
Yet I could not obtain it of myself   [Aside.
I'm so impatient to unfold the Riddle
Of Don Antonio's seeing of my Sister,
And entertaining her in her own Lodgings;
I shall not now be long i'the dark. O Heavens!
          [He sees her]
Tis she, herself, and Camilla with her:
Were all my servants mad; or all agreed
To abuse me, in affirming she was fled?
But Don Carlos, was he mad too, to swear
That he had traced her to another House?
Certainly I or they must be possessed;
Or some Enchantment reigns within these Walls.
   Ant. O here comes Don Henrique, now I'll
   acquaint him
With your sad Story, Madam.
   Cam. I fear we are undone.
   Ant. Don Henrique.
   Por. I'm dead if he proceed, but how to hinder him–

Ant. Here's a Lady with your Sister Porcia–
Hen. Yes, Sir, I see who 'tis.
Ant. Since you know her, Sir, you will the easier
Excuse my boldness.
Hen. Boldness! in what Sir?
Ant. To have been the occasion of your finding her
Here, with your Sister, at this time o'the night.
Hen. Lord Sir, what do you mean?
Ant. There was in truth such a necessity in it,
That 'twill, I hope, excuse my humble suit to you
In hers and my behalf.
Por. Now all comes out.
Hen. I understand you, Sir, she does desire
To pass this night with Porcia to assist her
In the ordering of her Nuptial Ceremonies:
Let her stay a God's Name.
Por. If he does not dissemble, my Condition
Is not so desperate as I imagined.   [Aside.
Ant. I hope you'll pardon this great Liberty;
So early a Confidence will need it, Sir.
Hen. Tis more than enough, that you desire it;
The occasion too does justify her stay.
Ant. Tis most true Sir, the occasion did enforce me
Thus boldly to presume upon your Friendship.
Hen. Ha' done for Heaven's sake, is it a Novelty
Think you for Porcia and her Cousin-German,
To pass a night together?
Ant. Is she so near a Kinswoman of his?
Strange inadvertence in her, not to tell me.
Her Relation to him, when I named him first.
I'd made fine work on't, had I told him all.   [Aside.
Hen. She knows I owe her many a good turn
          [Looking on the ladies, and spoken aside,
               so that Antonio might not hear him]
Upon Octavio's score, and hope ere long
To be able to repay her to the full.
Por. Can he declare his mind in plainer terms?
Cam. I cannot tell which of us two he means,
Those words may be applied to either of us,
But I begin to fear that he knows all.

Hen. Since 'tis so late, pray give the Ladies leave
To retire to their Chambers; Go in Sister,
Ant. My Brother's Words and his Behaviour
Imply some Mystery; but I must be silent
Till I discover more.   [Aside.
Por. Let us be gone, we're lost if we stay here;
I'm confident he counterfeits this Calm
To cover his Revenge, until Antonio,
And the rest of the House are gone to Bed.
Cam. But we shall ne'er be able to get out
Whil'st they continue in the outward Rooms.
Por. Yes, by the Garden door, but I'm afraid
Tis shut.
Cam. No, now I think on't, Flora went that way,
And left it open.
Por. Come, Let's be gone; I hope Heaven will ordain
Ease by that door, which first let in my pain.
                              [Exit Porcia and Camilla.

Ant. I'll only make a step Sir, to my Chamber,
And then return to you immediately.
Hen. Pray, Sir, give me leave to wait on you.
Ant. I humbly thank you, Sir, I know the way,
And shall not stay above a moment from you.
Hen. What you please, Sir, you command here.
Ant. I'll now go see whether my servant Sancho
Has brought Octavio to my Lodgings,
As I directed him.   [Aside.
                              [Exit Antonio.

Hen. Heavens! was there ever so strange a Mystery!
Don Carlos he affirmed that those we fought with
Had conveyed Porcia away; and when I come
To seek her in the House, I find her missing;
To second this, her Waiting-woman Flora
Tells me that she went down, about that time,
Into the Garden; Antonio, not long after,
Affirms that he both saw and entertained her,
In her own Apartment, where I now find her,
And Camilla with her: What can this be?

These sure are Riddles to pose an Oedipus;
But if by my own sense, I am assured
My Honour's safe, which was so much in doubt,
What matter is it how 'tis brought about?

                              [Exit Henrique.

ACT FIVE

(Outside) Don Carlos's house

[Enter Diego, Flora, and Pedro accompanying the chair,
groping as in the dark]

Ped. Dame Flora, and Signior Diego go in there.
And you, my Friends, set down the Chair, and let
The Lady out; Go, there's money for you.
I'll go fetch a Candle.

[Diego and Flora go in, and the chair being set in the door,
Octavio goes out into the room;
Pedro claps to the door and goes away]

The scene changes to inside Don Carlos's house

[Enter Octavio, Diego, Flora, at another door]

Oct. What! Put in all alone here i'the dark!
[Groping as in the dark]
And the door shut upon me! Diego, Flora.
Die. Here am I Sir, and Mistress Flora too.
Unless my Sense of feeling fails me.
Oct. I can't conjecture where we are; I durst not
So much as peep out of the Chair, since Flora
Gave me the warning; but wheree'er I am,
Tis better far than in the Sergeant's hands.
Flo. Though now i'the dark, I know well where we are;
I have too often walked the Streets, Octavio,
From your House hither, upon Cupid's Errands,
Not to know the Back-door of Carlos's
Apartment, 'tis there I am sure we are now.
Oct. Curse on thee, Flora! Had'st thou lost thy wits,

Not to let me know it sooner?

Die. A Gypsy told me by my Palm, long since,
A sour-faced Damsel should be my undoing.

Flo. Suspend awhile your Apprehensions, Sir;
You may escape before the Candles come;
The door was wont to open on this side;
If not, I have a way in store.

[Octavio goes to the door]

Oct. Flora, I cannot make the Lock go back.

[Pedro unlocks it on the other side, and coming in with a
Candle, meets with Octavio, and starting back and stumbling,
lets the Candle fall, then running out again, double-locks the
door]

Die. Nay then, i'faith, we're fast; I heard him give
The Key a double turn.

[Diego takes up the candle]

Here's a fair trial for your Maiden breath,
Flora blow it in again, let's owe your Mouth
More Light, than yet your Eyes could e'er impart.

Flo. Light's cast away on such an Owl as you.
But yet I'll try.

[Flora blows the Candle in]

Die. Thanks, gentle Flora, to your Virgin-Puff;
Tis a strong breath, that can o'ercome a Snuff.   [Aside.
But I had rather it had been let alone:
If I must needs be killed, unless it were
Behind my back, I'd have it i'the dark,
For I hate to be killed in my own presence.

Oct. What must we do Flora? all my hope's in you.

Flo. We've yet some room for hope; there's a Back-stair
Beyond that Inner Chamber, which goes down
Into the Garden, if the door be open,
As certainly it is, the way is easy.

Oct. Come, let's lose no time; prithee guide us, Flora
                                                          [Exeunt.

The scene changes to Don Henrique's house
[Enter Don Henrique]

Hen. As well pleased as I am, to find my Honour
Less desperate than I thought, I cannot rest
Till I have drawn from Porcia a Confession
Of the whole Truth, before she goes to bed;
She's in her Chamber now, unless by new
Enchantments carried thence.

[As he is going towards Porcia's chamber, enter
Carlos in haste]

Car. I can't imagine what should make Don Henrique
Quit the Corregidor's till we returned:
One of his servants tells me he's come home.
O here he is; now shall I raise a storm,
Which (if we do not take a special care)
Will scarce be allayed without a shower of Blood;
Yet I must venture it, since it so imports
Our Friendship, and the Honour of our House.

[Addressing Don Henrique]
Happiness is such a stranger to Mankind
That like forced Motion, it is ever strongest
At the first setting out, then languishing
With time, grows weary of our company;
But to Misfortunes we so subject are,
That like to Natural Motion they acquire
More force in their Progression.

Hen. What means this Philosophical Preamble?
Car. You'll know too soon, I fear.
Hen. Don Carlos, I am now so well recovered
From all my Inquietudes, that for the future,
I dare defy the malice of my Stars,
To cause a new Relapse into Distemper.

Car. Cousin, I'm much surprised with this great change,
But since you're such a Master of your Passions,
I'll spare my Ethics, and proceed to give you
In short the Narrative of our success;
Our worthy Kinsman the Corregidor,
Forward to serve you in the Affair I mentioned,
Was pleased to go along with me in Person,
With a strong Band of Sergeants, to the place
Where I, attended by your Servants, led him.

Cousin, 'twas there; it wounds my heart to speak it;
And I conjure you summon all your Patience,
'Twas there I found...
   Hen. Whom Cousin, did you find? for since I'm sure,
You found not Porcia there; my Concernments
In your Discoveries, are not very likely
To discompose me.
   Car. I would to Heaven we'd not found her there.
   Hen. What's that you say, Don Carlos; My Sister there!
   Car. Yes, Sir, your Sister.
   Hen. My Sister? that's good i'faith; ha, ha, ha.
   Car. Why do you laugh? Is the dishonour of
Our Family become a Laughing Matter?
This is a worse Extreme, methinks, than t'other.
   Hen. How can I choose but laugh to see you dream?
Awake for Heaven's sake; and recall your Senses.
Porcia there said you?
   Car. Yes Sir, Porcia I say; your Sister Porcia;
And which is more, 'twas in Octavio's House.
   Hen. Why sure you're not in earnest, Cousin.
   Car. As sure as you're alive I found her there.
   Hen. Then you transport me. Sir, beyond all Patience:
Why Cousin, if she has been still at home,
Antonio seen, and entertained her here,
Accompanied by Camilla; if even now
I left them there within; Is't possible
You should have found her in Octavio's House?
To be here, and there too, at the same time,
None sure but Janus with his double face
Can e'er unfold this Mystery.
   Car. Let me advise you, abuse not yourself;
I tell you positively I found her there;
And by the same token, her waiting-woman
Flora was there attending her.
   Hen. Flora? dear Cousin, do not still persist
Thus to affirm impossibilities.
   Car. Sure you are making some Experiment
Upon my Temper, and would fain provoke
My Patience, to some such high Disorder,
That I should ne'er hereafter have the face,

When you are in your Fits, to play the Stoic.

Hen. Cousin, I swear to you, upon my Honour,
Tis not above a quarter of an hour,
Since I did speak with Porcia and your Sister,
In that very Apartment, and am now
Returning to them in my Sister's Chamber.

Car. And Sir, I swear to you upon my Honour,
Tis not above a quarter of an hour,
Since I left Porcia carrying in a Chair,
From Don Octavio's House, and your Man Pedro
Leading the Chairmen to mine, and followed
By Flora, whil'st I came to find you out,
To acquaint you with this unpleasing News;
But fit for you to know, as soon as might be.

Hen. This Question, Cousin, may be soon decided;
Pray come along, her Chamber's not far off.

Car. And my House but the next door, let's go thither.

Hen. You'll quickly find your Error, Cousin.

Car. And you'll as soon be undeceived; but stay,
Here comes your Servant, whom I left to guard her;
He'll instantly convince you of the truth.

[Enter Pedro]

Ped. O Sir!...

Hen. What brings you hither, Pedro?

Ped. Give me my Albricias, Sir, I bring you
The rarest News, your Enemy, Octavio,
I'm quite out of breath...

Hen. What does the Varlet mean?

Ped. Sir, I suppose Don Carlos has informed you,
That he left me to see your Sister Porcia,
With Flora and Diego, Octavio's Man,
Safely conveyed to his House.

Car. See now Don Henrique, who was i'the right.

Ped. I did as he commanded me, and put them
All three into Don Carlos's Ante-Chamber,
Porcia in the same Chair, which brought her thither;
And for more safety double-lock'd the door,
Whil'st I went down in haste to fetch some Candles;

Hen. As sure as Death this Madness is infectious,

My Man is now in one of Carlos' Fits.

Ped. Returning with some Lights a moment after,
I no sooner opened the door, but Heavens!
Who should I see, there, standing Just before me,
In the selfsame place, where I left Porcia,
But Octavio, your Enemy Octavio.

Hen. Here is some Witchcraft, sure; what can this mean?

Ped. Amazed at this sight, I let the Candle fall:
And clapped the door to, then double-locked it,
And brought away the Key.

Car. But how could he get in, if you be sure
You locked the door, when you went out for Lights?

Ped. I know not whether he was there before,
Or got in after, but of this I'm sure,
That there I have him now, and safe enough.

Hen. Let's not, Don Carlos, now perplex ourselves
With needless Circumstances, when? and how?
Those Queries are too Flegmatic for me.
If the Beast be i'the toil it is enough;
Let us go seize him, for he must die.

[Enter Antonio]

Ant. Pray Brother, what unhappy man is he,
Whom you so positively doom to death?
I have a Sword to serve you, in all occasions,
Worthy of you, and me.

Hen. His intervening, Carlos, is unlucky,
How shall we behave ourselves towards him
In this Business so unfit for his knowledge?

[Carlos draws Henrique aside]

Car. Cousin, you should consider with yourself,
What answer to return him; he's not a Man
To be put off with any slight Pretence,
Nor yet to be engaged in such an Action,
As bears the appearance rather of Brutality
Than true Honour; you know, Antonio needs
No fresh Occasions to support his Name;
Who Dangers seek, are indigent of Fame.

Hen. I beg your patience Sir, but for one word

[Henrique addressing himself to Antonio]
With this Gentleman, my friend.
    Ant. I'll attend your leisure. I find my coming has disordered
    'em.
There's something they would fain conceal from me;
All here is discomposed, what e'er's the matter.   [Aside.
    Hen. I am a Rogue if I know what to do.
    Car. Since the Event's so dangerous and doubtlful.
Tis best, in my Opinion, Sir, to temporise.
    Hen. How easily men get the name of Wise!
To fear to engage, is called to temporize:
Sure Fear and Courage cannot be the same,
Yet they're confounded by a specious Name;
And I must tamely suffer, because Fools
Are ruled by nice Distinctions of the Schools.
How I hate such Cold Complexions.

[He stamps]

    Car. Why so transported, as if Vehemence
Were for your Passion an approved defence.
    Hen. Who condemns Passions, Nature he arraigns,
    Car. They're useful succours, when they serve in Chains;
But he who throws the Bridle on their Necks,
From a good Cause, will produce ill Effects.
    Hen. Be the Effects what they will, I am resolved.
[Addressing to Antonio]
I doubt not of your kind Concurrence, Sir,
In all the near Concernments of a Person
Allied to you, as I am; but noble Brother,
It were against the Laws of Hospitality
And Civil Breeding, to engage a Guest
(Newly arrived after so long a Journey)
In an occasion, where there may be danger.
    Ant. If such be the occasion, I must then
Acquaint you freely, that I wear a Sword,
Which must not be excluded from your Service;
I'm sure you are too Noble to employ yours
In any Cause, not justified by Honour.
    Hen. Though with Regret, I see, Sir, I must yield
To your excess of Generosity;

This only I shall say, to satisfy
Your just Reflections; that my Resentments
Are grounded on Affronts of such a Nature,
That as nothing but the Offender's life
Can e'er repair 'em, so as to the Forms
Of taking my Revenge, they can't admit
Of the least scruple.
    Ant. Honour's my Standard, and 'tis true, that I
Had rather Fall, than Blush for Victory;
But you are such a Judge of Honour's Laws,
That 'twere Injurious to suspect your Cause.
Allow me, Sir, the honour to lead the way.

                        [Exit Antonio and Henrique.

    Car. If Porcia be there too (as I believe)
'Twill prove, I fear, a fatal Tragedy;
But should she not be there; yet 'tis too much
For such a Heart as mine, through Ignorance
To have betrayed a Gentleman, though faulty,
Into such cruel hands; I must go with them;
But so resolved, as in this Bloody strife,
I'll save my Honour, or I'll lose my life.

                        [Exit Carlos.

       The scene changes to (inside) Don Carlos's house

       [Enter Octavio, Diego, Flora with a candle]

    Flo. O the unluckiness! I vow to you Sir,
I have scarce known that door e'er locked before.
    Oct. There's no Remedy Flora, I am now
At the mercy of my Enemies.
    Die. Having broken into another's ground,
Tis just, i'faith, you should be put i'the Pound.
    Oct. The Tide of my ill Fate is swollen so high,
'Twill not admit increase of misery;
Since amongst all the Curses, there is none
So wounds the spirit, as Privation.
For 'tis not where we lie, but whence we fell,
The loss of Heaven's the greatest Pain in Hell;

When I had sailed the doubtful Course of Love,
Had safely gained my Port, and far above
My Hopes, the precious Treasure had secured,
For which so many storms I had endured;
To be so soon from this great Blessing torn;
That's hard to say, if 'twere first Dead, or Born,
May doubtless seem such a transcendent Curse,
That even the Fates themselves, could do no worse;
Yet this I bore with an erected face,
Since Fortune, not my Fault caused my Disgrace;
But now, my Eyes unto the Earth are bent,
Conscious of meriting this Punishment;
For trusting a fond Maid's officious Care,
My Life and Honour's taken in this Snare;
And thus I perish, on this unseen Shelf,
Pursued by Fate, and false unto myself.
Flora, When I am dead, I pray present
           [He pulls out his Tablets]
These Tablets to your Lady, there she'll find,
My last Request, with Reasons which I give
That for my sake, she would vouchsafe to live.
Give me the Candle, Flora.

    [Octavio sets the candle on a table, and sits down
             to write in his tablets]

  Die. A double Curse upon all Love in earnest,
All Constant Love; 'tis still accompanied
With strange Disasters; or else ends in that
Which is the worst of all Disasters, Marriage.
  Flo. Sure you could wish that everybody living
Had such a Soul of Quicksilver, as yours,
That can fix nowhere.
  Die. Why 'twould not be the worse for you, dear Flora,
You then might hope in time to have your Turn,
As well as those who have much better Faces.
  Flo. You, I presume Sir, would be one o'the latest
Which I should hear of, yet 'tis possible
That one might see you, before you should be Welcome.
  Die. She has Wit and good Humour, excellent
Ingredients to pass away the time;

And I have kindness for her Person too;
But that will end with Marriage, and possibly
Her good Humour; for I have seldom known
The Husband and the Wife make any Music,
Though when asunder they can play their parts.
Well, friend Diego, I advise you to look
Before you leap, for if you should be coupled
To a Yolk, instead of a Yolk-fellow,
Tis likely you may wear it to your Grave.
Yet, honest Diego, now I think on't better,
Your Dancing and your Vaulting days are done;
Faith, all your Pleasures are three Stories high,
They are come up to your Mouth; you are now
For Ease and Eating, the only Joys of Life;
And there's no Cook, nor Dry-Nurse like a Wife.

    Oct. Here take my Tablets, Flora; sure they'll spare
Thy life for thy Sex's sake; but for poor Diego...

    Die. Why Sir, they'll never offer to kill me,
There's nothing in the world I hate like death.

    Oct. Since Death's the passage to Eternity,
To be for ever Happy, we must die.

    Die. Tis very true; but most that die would live,
If to themselves they could new Leases give.

    Oct. We must possess our Souls with such indifference,
As not to Wish, nor Fear to part from hence.

    Die. The first I may pretend to, for I swear
I do not wish to part; 'tis true I fear.

    Oct. Fear! why, Death's only cruel when he flies,
And will not deign to close the Weeping Eyes.

    Die. That is a Cruelty I can forgive,
For I confess I'm not afraid to live.

    Oct. We shall still live, though 'tis by others' breath,
By our good Fame, which is secured by Death.

    Die. But we shall catch such Colds, Sir, underground,
That we shall never hear Fame's Trumpet sound.

    Oct. Tis but returning, when from hence we go,
As Rivers to their Mother Ocean flow.

    Die. We know our Names and Channels whilst we're here,
We're swallowed in that dark Abyss when there.

    Oct. Engulfed in endless Joys and perfect Rest,

Unchangeable, i'the Centre of the Blessed.
Die. Hark, I hear a noise.

[The noise of the opening of a door. Diego runs to the door,
  looks into the next room, then comes running to Octavio]

O Sir, we're lost, I see two Female Giants
Coming most terribly upon us.
Oct. Away you fearful Fool.

[Enter Camilla and Porcia, the one with a key,
          the other with a candle]

Por. I'm confident nobody saw us pass
From the other House.
Cam. However, let' s go through my Brother's Quarter,
And open the Backdoor into the Street,
Tis good in all Events to have a Retreat
More ways than one.

[A door claps behind, and both look back]

Por. O Heavens! our surest passage is cut off,
The wind has shut the door through which we came.
Cam. The Accident's unlucky, 'tis a Spring-Lock,
That opens only on the other side.
Por. Let's on the faster, and make sure of t'other.
Octavio here!

[Seeing Octavio she starts. Octavio hearing them starts up]

Oct. Porcia in this place! may I trust my Senses,
Or does my Fancy form these Chimeras?
Die. Either we sleep, and dream extravagantly,
Or else the Fairies govern in this House.

[Flora runs to Porcia]

Flo. Ah! Dearest Mistress, you shall never make me
Quit you so again.
Por. But can that be Octavio?
Oct. I was Octavio, but I am at present
So much astonished, I am not myself.
Cam. What can the meaning of this Vision be?

[Octavio approaches Porcia]

Oct. My dearest Porcia, how is't possible
To find you in this place, my Friend Antonio
Having so generously undertaken
Your Protection?
    Por. Did he not yours so too? and yet I find
Octavio here, where he is more exposed
Than I, to certain ruin; I am loth
To say 'tis he who has betrayed us both.
    Oct. Antonio false? it is impossible.
    Die. Tis but too evident.
    Oct. Peace Slave; he is my Friend, of Noble Blood,
Whose Fame's above the level of those Tongues,
That bark by Custom at the brightest Virtues,
As Dogs do at the Moon.
    Por. How hard it is for Virtue to suspect.
Ah Octavio! We have been both deceived;
This vile Antonio is the very Man,
To whom my Brother, without my consent,
Or knowledge, has contracted me in Flanders.
    Oct. Antonio the Man to whom you are contracted?
Porcia the Bride, whom he is come to marry?
    Por. The very same.
    Oct. Why did you not acquaint me with it sooner?
    Por. Alas, I have not seen you since I knew it;
But those few hours such wonders have produced,
As exceed all belief; and ask more time
Than your unsafe condition in this place,
Will allow me, to make you comprehend it.
    Cam. Cousin, I cannot blame your apprehensions,
Nor your Suspicion of Antonio's Friendship:
But I am so possessed with the opinion
Of his Virtue, I shall as soon believe
Impossibilities, as his Apostacy
From Honour.
    Oct. What's her Concernment in Antonio, Porcia?
    Por. O that's the strangest part of our sad Story,
And which requires most time to let you know it.

[A blaze of light appears at the window, and a noise without]

    Por. See, Flora, at the Window, what's that Light

And noise we hear.

[Flora goes to the window].

Flo. O Madam! we are all undone, I see
Henrique, Carlos, and their Servants, with Torches,
All coming hither; and which is wonderful,
Antonio leading them with his Sword drawn.
    Cam. Thou dream'st, distracted Wench; Antonio false?
It is impossible.
[Camilla runs to the Window, and turning back says]
All she has said is in appearance true,
There's sure some hidden Mystery, which thus
Abuses us; for I shall ne'er believe
Antonio can transgress the Rules of Friendship.
    Oct. Friendship's a specious Name, made to deceive
Those, whose Good Nature tempts them to believe;
The Traffic of good Offices 'mongst Friends,
Moves from ourselves, and in ourselves it ends.
When Competition brings us to the test,
Then we find Friendship is self-interest.
    Por. Ye Powers above! What pleasure can ye take
To persecute Submitting Innocence?
    Oct. Retire, dear Porcia, to that inner Room,
For should thy Cruel Brother find thee here,
He's so revolted from Humanity,
He'll mingle thine, with my Impurer Blood.
    Por. That were a kind of Contract; let him come,
We'll meet at once Marriage and Martyrdom.
    Oct. Soul of my life, retire.
    Por. I will not leave you.
    Oct. Thou preserv'st me by saving of thyself;
For they can murder only half of me,
Whil'st that my better part survives in thee.
    Por. I will die too, Octavio, to maintain
That different Causes form the same Effects;
Tis Courage in you Men, Love in our Sex.
    Oct. Though Souls no Sexes have, when we're above,
If we can know each other, we may love.
    Por. I'll meet you there above, here take my word.

[Octavio takes her hand and kisses it]

This Porcia knows, the way of joining Souls,
As well as t'other, when she swallowed coals.

[They retire to the other room, Porcia leaning on Camilla,
        and Octavio waits on them to the door]

Die. Nay if you're good at that, the Devil take
The hindmost; 'tis for your sake fair Flora
                    [Taking Flora by the hand]
I shun these honourable occasions.
                        [Turning to Octavio]
Having no Weapon, Sir, 'tis fit that I
March off with the Baggage.

                                    [Exit Diego, Flora.

Oct. I'm now upon the Frontiers of this Life.
There's but one step to Immortality;
And since my cruel Fortune has allowed me
No other witness of my Tragic end,
But a false Friend and Barbarous Enemy,
I'll leave my Genius to inform the World,
My Life and Death was uniform; as I
Lived firm to Love and Honour, so I die.
                    [Draws his sword]
Look down ye Spirits above, for, If there be
A sight on Earth worthy of you to see,
Tis a brave Man pursued by injust hate,
Bravely contending with his adverse Fate.
                    [Waving his sword]
Stay till this Heaven-born soul puts off her Earth,
And she'll attend ye to her place of Birth.

        [Enter Antonio, Henrique, Carlos, and Pedro, their
            swords drawn, Antonio before the rest]

Ant. Where is the Man whose Insolence and Folly
Has so misled him to affront my Friend?
Oct. Here is the Man thou seek'st, and he, whom thou
So basely hast betrayed.
Ant. Oh Heavens! what is't I see? it is Octavio,

My Friend.

Oct. Not thy Friend, Antonio, but 'tis Octavio,
Who by thy Perfidy has been betrayed
To this forlorn Condition; but Vile Man,
Thou now shalt pay thy Treachery with thy Life.

[Octavio makes at Antonio]

Ant. Hold Octavio, though thy Injurious Error
May transport thee, it shall not me, beyond
The Bounds of Honour; Heaven knows I thought
Of nothing less, than what I find, Octavio
In this place.

Hen. What pause is this, Antonio; All your Fervour
In the Concernments of a Brother-in-Law,
Reduced to a tame Parley with our Enemy?
Do all the Promises you've made to me,
To assist my just Revenge, conclude in this?

Oct. Do all the Promises you've made to me,
T'assist my virtuous Love, conclude in this?

Hen. Where is your wonted Bravery? Where your
Kindness?
To such a near Ally?

Oct. Where is your former Honour? Where your Firmness?
To such an ancient Friend?

Ant. What course shall my Distracted Honour steer,
Betwixt these equal opposite Engagements?   [Aside.

Hen. What, demur still? Nay then I'll right myself.

[Henrique makes at Octavio, Antonio turns on Octavio's side]

Ant. Who attacks Octavio, must pass through me.

Car. I must lay hold on this occasion.   [Aside.
Good Cousin, I conjure you to restrain
Your Passion for a while, there lies concealed
Some Mystery in this, which once unfolded,
May Reconcile this Difference.

Hen. Sweetly proposed, Sir, an Accommodation?
Think'st thou my Anger's like a Fire of Straw,
Only to Blaze, and then Expire in Smoke?
Think'st thou I can forget my Name and Nation,
And barter for Revenge, when Honour Bleeds?

His Life must pay this Insolence, or mine.

[He makes at Octavio again. Antonio interposes]

Ant. Mine must protect his, or else perish with him.
Hen. Since neither Faith nor Friendship can prevail,
Tis time to try what proof you are, Antonio,
Against your own near Interest; Know that Man,
Whom you protect against my just Revenge,
Has seconded his Insolence to me
By foul Attempts upon my Sister's honour;
Your Porcia's, Sir. If this will not enflame you...

[Antonio turns from Octavio, and beholds him
with a stern countenance]

Oct. How! I attempt your Sister's Honour, Henrique?
The Parent of your black Designs, the Devil,
Did ne'er invent a more malicious Falsehood;
Tis true, that I have served the Virtuous Porcia,
With Such Devotion, and such spotless Love,
That, though unworthy, yet she has been pleased
To recompense my Passion with Esteem
[Antonio turns and looks sternly upon Octavio]
By which, she has so chained me to her service,
That here I vow either to live her Prize,
Or else in Death to fall Love's Sacrifice.
Ant. O Heavens! what's that I hear? Thou blessed Angel,
Guardian of my Honour, I now implore
Thy powerful assistance, to preserve
That Reputation, which I hitherto
By Virtuous Actions have maintained unblemished.
[He pauses a little and rubs his forehead]
In vain, Don Henrique you design to change
My resolutions, it must ne'er be said,
That Passion could turn Antonio
From the strict Rules of Honour; Sir, I tell you
Nothing can make me violate my first
Engagement.
Hen. Nay, then, thou shall die too, Perfidious Man;
Ho! Geraldo, Pedro, Leonido.

[Enter Geraldo, Pedro, Leonido, with their swords drawn,
and join with Henrique. Carlos interposes]

Car. For Heaven's sake, Cousin, draw not on yourself
The horrid Infamy of Assassinating
Persons of Noble Blood, by servile Hands.
 Hen. Do you defend them too? Kill 'em I say.
 Ant. Retire Octavio, I'll sustain their shock.
 Oct. Octavio retire?
 Ant. Trust me you must, they will surround us else;
Through that narrow Passage they'll assail us
With less advantage.

[They retire fighting off the stage, Henrique and his men
pursuing them, and Carlos endeavouring to stop Don Henrique]

 Hen. What d'ye give back, ye men of mighty Fame?
 Ant. Don Henrique, you shall quickly find, 'tis Honour,
Not Fear, makes me retire.

           [Exeunt.

[Enter presently Antonio and Octavio at another
door, which Antonio bolts]

 Ant. Now we shall have a breathing while at least,
Octavio, and time to look about us;
Pray see yon other Door be fast.

[Octavio steps to the door where they went out
and Henrique bounces at the door they came in at]

 Hen. (within) Pray Geraldo, fetch an Iron Bar to force the
Door.

[Antonio goes to both the doors, to see if they be fast]

 Ant. So, 'tis now as I would wish it;
 Oct. What do you mean, most Generous Antonio?
 Ant. To kill thee now myself; having performed
What my Engagement did exact from me
In your defence 'gainst others; my Love now
Requires its Dues, as Honour has had his;
There's no Protection for you from my Sword,
But in your own, or in your frank Renouncing

All Claim to Porcia; she is so much mine,
That none must Breathe, and have the Vanity
Of a Pretender to her, whil'st I live.

    Oct. I never will Renounce my Claims to Porcia;
But still assert them by all noble ways:
Yet, Sir, this hand shall never use a Sword
(Without the last Compulsion) 'gainst that Man
Who has so much obliged me; no, Antonio,
You are securely Guarded by the Favours
Which you so frankly have conferred upon me.

    Ant. Pray, Sir, let not pretended Gratitude
Enervate your Defence; 'tis not my Custom
To serve my Friends with Prospects of Return.

    Oct. And, Sir, 'tis not my Custom to receive
An Obligation, but with a purpose,
And within the Power of my Return.
Friendship, Antonio, is reciprocal,
He that will only Give, and not Receive,
Enslaves the Person whom he would Relieve.

    Ant. Your Rule is right, but you apply it wrong,
It was Octavio, my Comrade in Arms,
And ancient Friend, whom I designed to serve;
Not that Disloyal Man, who has invaded
My Honour and my Love: 'Tis the Intent
Which forms the Obligation, not the Event.

    Oct. I call those Powers, who both discern and punish,
To witness for me, that I never knew
You e'er pretended to Don Henrique's Sister,
Before I came within these fatal Walls:
This I declare, only to clear myself,
From the Imputation of Disloyalty,
And to prevent the Progress of your Error.

    Ant. How can I think you should speak truth to me,
Who am a Witness you've been false to her,
To whom you now profess so high Devotion.

    Oct. I false to Porcia.? Take heed, Antonio!
So foul an Injury provokes too much;
But, Sir, I must confess I owe you more,
Than the Forgiveness of one gross Mistake.

    Ant. Rare Impudence! I must not trust my Senses.

Oct. If we cannot adjust this Competition,
Let's charge our envious Fortunes, not our Passions,
With this fatal breach of Friendship.
    Ant. Leave your discourses and defend yourself.
Either immediately renounce all Claims
To Porcia, or this must speak the rest.

[Shaking his sword]

Oct. Nay, then, this must reply.

[They fight]

[A noise as if the door were broken open]

[Enter Henrique, Carlos, Leonido, Geraldo with their swords
drawn]

    Hen. What's this! Antonio fighting with Octavio?
This Bravery is excessive, Gallant Friend,
Not to allow a share in your Revenge
To him, who's most concerned; he must not fall
Without some Marks of mine.

[Henrique makes at Octavio, and Antonio
turns to Octavio's side]

    Ant. Nay, then my Honour you invade anew,
And by assaulting him, revive in me
My Pre-engagements to protect and serve him
Against all others.
    Hen. Why, were not you, Antonio, fighting with him?
Were you not doing all you could, to kill him?
    Ant. Henrique, 'tis true, but finding in my Breast
An equal strife 'twixt Honour and Revenge,
I do in just compliance with them both
Preserve him from your Sword, to fall by mine.
    Car. Brave Man, how nicely he does Honour weigh!
Justice herself holds not the Scales more even.
    Hen. My Honour suffers more, as yet, than yours,
And I must have my share in the Revenge.
    Ant. My Honour, Sir, is so sublimed by Love,
'Twill not admit Comparison or Rival.

Hen. Either he must renounce all Claims to Porcia,
Or die immediately.

Ant. You're i'the right, that he must do, or die:
But by no other hand than mine.

Oct. Cease your Contention, and turn all your Swords
Against this Breast; whil'st Porcia and I have breath,
She must be mine, there's no Divorce but Death.

Hen. I'll hear no more, protect him if thou canst;
Kill the Slave, kill him, I say.

[Henrique makes at him, and Carlos endeavours to interpose]

Car. For Heaven's sake hold a Moment! Certainly
There's some mistake lies hidden here, which cleared,
Might hinder these Extremes.

[Henrique and his servants press Antonio and Octavio.
Flora peeps out, and seeing them fight cries out]

Flo. Camilla! Porcia!

[Camilla and Porcia looking out, both shriek and then run
out upon the stage]

Por. Don Henrique!

Cam. Antonio! Carlos!

Por. Octavio!

Cam. and Por. Hear us but speak, hear us but speak.

Hen. By Heavens 'tis Porcia! Why how came she here?

Car. Why did not I tell you she was brought hither
By my Directions? you would not believe me.

Hen. But how then could Octavio come hither?

Car. Nay, that Heaven knows; you heard as well as I
Your Man's Relation.

Hen. Ah, thou Vile Woman, that I could destroy
Thy Memory, with thy Life.

[He offers to run at Porcia. Antonio interposes]

Ant. Hold, Sir, that must not be.

Hen. What, may not I do Justice upon her
Neither?

Ant. No Sir; although I have not yet the Honour
To know who this Lady is, I have this Night

Engaged myself, both to secure and serve her.

Car. He knows not Porcia; who was i'the right,
Don Henrique, you, or I?

Hen. He not know Porcia? why 'tis not an hour,
Since I saw him entertaining her at home;
Sure we're enchanted, and all we see's Illusion.

Cam. Allow me, Henrique, to unspell these charms;
Who is't, Octavio, you pretend to? Speak.

Oct. You might have spared that question, Madam, none
Knows so well as you, 'tis Porcia I adore.

Ant. Porcia's my Wife; Disloyal Man thou diest.

[Offers to make at Octavio]

Cam. Hold Sir, which is the Porcia you lay claim too?

Ant. Can you doubt that? why sure you know too well
The Conquest that you made so long ago,
Of my poor heart in Flanders.

Car. Conquest! poor heart! Flanders! what can this
mean?

Hen. New Riddles every moment do arise,
And Mysteries are born of Mysteries.

Car. Sure, 'tis the Pastime of the Destinies
To mock us, for pretending to be wise.

Cam. Thanks be to Heaven, our work draws near an end.
Cousin, it belongs to you to finish it.

Por. To free you from that Labyrinth, Antonio,
In which a slight mistake, not rectified,
Involved us all, know, the supposed Porcia,
Whom you so long have loved's the true Camilla.

Cam. And you, Don Henrique, know, that Don
Octavio
Has always been your Sister's faithful Lover,
And only feigned a Gallantry to me,
To hide his real passion for my Cousin
From your discerning eyes.

Ant. Generous Octavio.

Oct. Brave Antonio, how happy are we both!
Both in our Loves and Friendships!

[They embrace]

Ant. Ah! how the memory of our Crosses past,
Heightens our joys when we succeed at last.

Oct. Our pleasures in this world are always mixed.
Tis in the next where all our joys are fixed.

[Camilla takes Antonio by the hand,
and leads him to Don Carlos]

Cam. This, my dear Brother, is that brave Commander,
To whom you owe your Life and Liberty;
And I much more, the safety of my Honour.

Car. Is this that Gallant Leader, who redeemed us
With so much Valour from the Enemy?

Cam. The very same!

Car. Why did you not acquaint me with it sooner?
'Twas ill done Camilla.

Cam. Alas, my dearest Brother, Gratitude
                    [Drawing Carlos aside]
Conspiring with the Graces of his Person,
So soon possessed him of my Heart, that I
Ashamed of such a Visionary Love,
Durst never trust my Tongue with my own Thoughts.

Car. Tis enough. Here Sir, take from me her Hand
                    [Addressing to Antonio]
Whose Heart, your Merit has long since made yours.

[Antonio takes Camilla's hand and kisses it]

Ant. Sir, with your leave, and hers, I seal the Vows
Of my Eternal Faith, unto you both.

Car. But let's take heed, Antonio, least whilst we
Are joying in our mutual happiness,
Don Henrique's scarcely yet composed Distemper
Revive not, and disorder us afresh:
I like not his grim posture.

Ant. Tis well thought on, let's approach him.

[Octavio holding Porcia by the hand,
advances towards Henrique]

Oct. Here, with respect, we wait your Confirmation
Of that, which seems to be decreed above,
Though traversed by unlucky Accidents.

This Lady, your Incomparable Sister,
Can witness, that I never did invade
Your passion for Camilla; and Pedro's death
Happened by your mistaken Jealousy.
The Causes of your Hate being once removed,
Tis just, Don Henrique, the Effects should cease.
 Hen. I shall consult my Honour.
 Car. You cannot take a better Counsellor
In this Case, than your own and Sister's Honour;
What, to secure them both, could have been wished
Beyond what Fate has of itself produced?
 Hen. How hard it is to act upon Constraint!
That which I could have wished, I now would fly;
Since 'tis obtruded by Necessity.
Tis fit that I consent, but yet I must
Still seem displeased, that my Anger may seem just.
 Ant. Noble Don Henrique you may reckon me
To be as truly yours, by this Alliance,
As if a Brother's Name subsisted still.
 Hen. Well, I must yield, I see, or worse will follow.
He is a Fool who thinks by force, or skill,   [Aside.
To turn the Current of a Woman's Will.
Since fair Camilla is Antonio's Lot,
I Porcia yield to Don Antonio's Friend.
Our Strength and Wisdom must submit to Fate,
Stripped of my Love, I will put off my Hate.
Here, take her hand, and may she make you, Sir,
Happier than she has done me.

> [Henrique takes Porcia by the hand and gives her
> to Octavio. Diego and Flora advance]

 Flo. Had e'er Disorders such a rare come-off?
Methinks t'would make a fine Plot for a Play.
 Die. Faith Flora, I should have the worst of that;
For by the Laws of Comedy, it would be
My Lot to marry you.
 Oct. Well thought on, Diego, though 'tis spoke in jest;
We cannot do a better thing, in earnest,
Than to join these, who seem to have been made
For one another. What say'st thou to it. Flora?

Flo. Troth, I have had so many frights this night,
That I am e'en afraid to lie alone.

[Diego takes her by the hand]

Die. Give me thy hand sweet Flora, 'tis a Bargain,
I promise thee, dear Spouse, I'll do my best
To make thee, first, repent this earnest jest.
Flo. You may mistake; we have a certain way
By going halves, to match your foulest play.
Car. Since this last happy Scene is in my House,
You'll make Collation with me ere ye part.
Ant. and Oct. Agreed, agreed, agreed.
Ant. Thus ends the strange Adventures of Five Hours;
As sometimes Blustering Storms, in Gentle Showers.
Oct. (To the pit) Thus Noble Gallants, after Blustering Lives,
You'll end, as we have done, in taking Wives.
Die. Hold Sirs! there's not an end as yet, for then,
Comes your own Brats, and those of other Men.
Hen. Besides the cares of the honour of your Race,
Which, as you know, is my accursed Case.
Cam. (To the Boxes) You Ladies, whil'st unmarried, tread on
snares,
Married, you're cumbered with Domestic Cares.
Por. If handsome, you're by Fools and Fame attacked;
If ugly, then, by your own Envy racked.
Flo. We, by unthrifty Parents forced to serve,
When fed are Slaves; and when we're free, we starve.
Car. Which put together, we must needs confess,
This World is not the Scene of Happiness.

THE END

Paul Hopkins has combined journalism with the theatre throughout his career, occasionally to the extreme of reviewing shows in which he was also appearing. While working for newspapers and magazines he acted at the Maddermarket and Unity Theatres, directed amateur companies and campaigned for the building of the Harlow Playhouse. His history of the arts in the new town, *The Long and the Short and the Tall*, was described as 'a fascinating story, interestingly compiled' by Peter Hepple in *The Stage*.

He now combines journalism training with editing and staging Shakespearean adaptations by Dryden, Davenant, Shadwell, Tate and others at Royal Shakespeare Company Summer Schools at Stratford. It was this interest which led him to Samuel Tuke's adaptation of a Spanish play.